W9-BTR-621

BUTTERFLIES
OF THE PACIFIC NORTHWEST

By William Neill

Photography by Doug Hepburn and William Neill

2007
Mountain Press Publishing Company
Missoula, Montana

© 2007 William Neill

Photography by Doug Hepburn and William Neill

Front cover photo by Doug Hepburn:
Male Mormon Fritillaries (*Speyeria mormonia*)

Back cover photos by William Neill:
Mourning Cloak eggs (*Nymphalis antiopa*)
Anise Swallowtail caterpillar (*Papilio zelicaon*)
Leanira Checkerspot pupa (*Thessalia leanira*)
Acmon Blue butterly (*Plebejus acmon*)

Library of Congress Cataloging-in-Publication Data

Neill, William, 1929–
  Butterflies of the Pacific Northwest / by William Neill ; photography by Doug
Hepburn and William Neill.
      p. cm.
  Includes index.
  ISBN 978-0-87842-537-2 (pbk. : alk. paper)
  1. Butterflies—Northwest, Pacific—Identification. 2. Butterflies—Northwest,
Pacific—Pictorial works. I. Hepburn, Doug. II. Title.
QL551.N67N443 2007
595.78'909795—dc22
                          2007021882

                    PRINTED IN HONG KONG

                Mountain Press Publishing Company
            P.O. Box 2399 • Missoula, Montana 59806
            406-728-1900 • www.mountain-press.com

CONTENTS

AUTHOR'S NOTE

This book is an expanded version of my book *The Guide to Butterflies of Oregon and Washington*, published by Westcliffe Publishers in 2001, now out of print. But *version* is the wrong word—it's more like the final stage of the earlier book's metamorphosis. This book is as different from the old one as a butterfly is from its caterpillar.

Since the earlier book came into readers' hands, I've had opportunities to learn about its strengths and weaknesses, especially during numerous field trips I conducted through the Audubon Society of Portland. Watching the way people used that book gave me ideas for some important changes in this one, *Butterflies of the Pacific Northwest*.

New species. Eighteen additional butterfly species have been added to the hundred species in the former book. There are now 118 species shown and described in detail—almost all the species you're likely to encounter in this area.

More butterfly photos. The original book generally relied on just one butterfly photo to illustrate a species. We've added multiple views for many species—for example, top as well as underside, male and female— for easier field identification. Now there are 175 adult butterfly photos for the 118 species.

More caterpillars. Many butterfly enthusiasts wanted to see more about the immature stages of the butterfly's life cycle. This book includes color photographs of 57 species of caterpillars.

More photos in general. Eggs, caterpillars, pupae, butterflies, their habitats, the works: 312 photos in all.

Butterflies of the Pacific Northwest contains more to engage the serious student but retains the essential character of the earlier book. It's still aimed primarily at people who have an interest in nature and want a book that will help them learn more about the butterflies they see in this part of the country. *Butterflies of the Pacific Northwest* is easy to use. No prior expertise is needed, just curiosity.

WILLIAM NEILL

Silvery Blue

SPECIES LIST

This is a list of the 118 species of butterflies described in this book. The list does not include every species ever discovered in the Pacific Northwest, but it does include most that you are likely to encounter. As many as 170 to 180 species have been reported in the region at one time or another, the exact number depending on how you define the region's borders.

The 118 species are arranged in fifteen groups based mainly on established scientific classification, even though the names of the groups sometimes differ from the scientific family names for butterflies. The exception is the Aristocrats. I placed members of this group together because they share physical characteristics that make them recognizable in the field, such as large size and bright color patterns.

Butterfly names have changed over time and doubtless will continue to change, and not all lepidopterists agree on the most suitable names to be used at present for some species. I've attempted to use the most widely accepted names in this book, but some of my choices are arbitrary. When in doubt, I've followed Pyle's authoritative *Butterflies of Cascadia*. I've also tried to avoid confusion by including the alternative names for some butterflies.

Lepidopterists have subdivided many of these species into subspecies. For the sake of simplicity, I treat each species as a unit and do not consider subspecies. In the few instances in which I mention subdivisions of a species, I usually use the term *variety*.

HOW TO USE THIS BOOK

In the Introduction of this book you can learn how butterflies live their lives and get along with the rest of the natural world—what makes them tick. The Species Accounts section following the Introduction describes 118 species of butterflies you can find in the Pacific Northwest. By reading in that sequence, you can first soak up some facts about butterflies in general, then begin sorting out the ones you'll be seeing in your own area.

You can also skip the Introduction and head right for the color photographs, using the book simply as a field guide for identification. In this case, have a look at the Species List (page ix) to familiarize yourself with the butterflies you may come across, and perhaps check the Quick Guide located inside the front cover. Be sure to study the drawing of a butterfly's wings and the explanation of the descriptive terms used in the Species Accounts, both found on page 42. In addition, check out Telling Males from Females on page 175. Sooner or later, I hope, your curiosity will bring you back to try the introductory text. If you understand more of what butterflies do, you'll be able to see much more of what is out there when you venture back into the field.

WILLIAM NEILL

Leanira Checkerspot

___ ABOUT THE PHOTOGRAPHS___

Doug Hepburn and William Neill took the photographs in this book with an Olympus camera mounted with a zoom lens and either a bellows or a fixed lens extender. This is a compact, lightweight setup suitable for pursuing a mobile target. They used Kodachrome ASA 25 or 64 film and depended exclusively on ambient sunlight, preferring its natural look and unmanipulated presentation of the butterflies in their surroundings. Without flash lighting, the fine-grained slow film limited the workable exposure settings. Aperture f8 at 1/60 second was typical. Butterflies usually don't pose long for their portrait, so the camera was handheld, with an elbow braced against the ground or a knee for stability. For pictures of eggs or pupae, they often used a tripod.

They shot as many photographs of each species as they could and selected the ones that most clearly demonstrated its unique features. With some butterflies, the most important field marks are on the top surface of the wings; in others, on the underside; and in some cases, it's best to view both surfaces. They gave preference to pictures showing butterflies engaged in some interesting activity. Finally, the aesthetic merits of a picture were taken into account.

INTRODUCTION

About Butterflies in General

WHAT IS A BUTTERFLY?

The animal kingdom is dominated by two principal groups: vertebrates and arthropods. The soft body of vertebrate animals (including humans) is slung from a rigid internal skeleton. In contrast, the skeleton of arthropods, including butterflies, is on the outside, like a shell. The hard external skeleton, or exoskeleton, of arthropods provides protection and defines their shape, holding the soft parts in place. Ancestors of these two groups diverged when animals were at a primitive stage of development, and the fantastic array of species that now exists among vertebrates (all fish, amphibians, reptiles, birds, and mammals) and arthropods (all insects, spiders, and crustaceans) appears to be the outcome of branching and rebranching along two separate evolutionary paths.

In addition to their exoskeleton, another characteristic of arthropods is jointed legs. An arthropod with six jointed legs is an insect. Spiders, crabs, and centipedes are examples of arthropods with more than six legs. The insect model has shown great evolutionary flexibility in adapting to the earth's varied environmental niches. More than half of known animal species are insects.

In regard to their functional capabilities, insects can accomplish complex activities through industriousness and persistence. As species, they also adapt well over generations to environmental change. As individuals, they appear to operate according to rigid stereotypical behavior, or instinct. Even though its behavior may be complex, an individual insect does not react in a resourceful manner when faced with new, unexpected circumstances.

Some insects have wings covered by scales; they are called Lepidoptera, which means "scaly wings." Lepidoptera are separated into two groups: butterflies and moths. The feature that most reliably distinguishes one group from the other is the antennae. In butterflies, the antennae terminate with knobs (the knob is drawn out into a curved point in skipper butterflies). The antennae of moths taper to a point. Other differences are less reliable for telling the two groups apart. The bodies of butterflies are usually more slender and less "furry" than those of moths. Unlike moths, butterflies seldom fly at night.

SPECIES AND VARIATION

Animals that mate with each other and produce viable and fertile offspring are members of the same species. This is not the only definition of *species,*but

1

it's a useful one. What keeps the borders of a species intact? Members of a species generally don't mate with other species. They exchange and mix genetic material only with each other. Even so, you will see some small variation in physical characteristics from one individual to the next within a single species. The physical differences between separate species, however, are usually more pronounced—large enough to differentiate even closely related species. Anglewings, tortoiseshells, and admirals are butterfly species with a relatively consistent appearance. There is much more variation among fritillaries and checkerspots, sometimes making it difficult to determine the species of an individual butterfly.

Another type of variation occurs in some species: individuals in one geographic area look different from those in another. For example, the whole population of Mormon Fritillaries in the Ochoco Mountains has shiny silver spots on the wings. Not so for Mormon Fritillaries on Steens Mountain 100 miles to the south. There the spots are dull yellow. This is a consistent finding. You'd never mistake a Mormon Fritillary from Steens for one from the Ochocos.

Butterfly colonies that are isolated from each other lose the opportunity for interbreeding because most butterflies don't fly long distances. Over many generations, an isolated colony may evolve its own peculiarities, such as different spots. The two colonies inhabiting the Ochoco Mountains and Steens Mountain aren't really separate species—given the opportunity, the two groups could probably breed—but they're visually distinct from each other. Different colonies are sometimes referred to as separate subspecies, or varieties of the same species.

How unique must a colony be to earn the title of subspecies? After all, minor differences between local populations of a given species are common, almost ubiquitous. Should there be separate names for each one? Sometimes there is more debate than consensus among experts about naming subspecies. The main point to keep in mind is that ordinary variability within a species occurs on the same piece of land where individuals are routinely mating and mixing genes. Subspecies require reproductive isolation, usually geographic.

The total range of most butterfly species is not extensive. The eastern and western edges of the United States each have their own species list, with an overlap of only about 20 percent. Even within its geographic range, a species may be found only in isolated colonies, with individuals seldom wandering into intervening, less suitable territory.

More than 10,000 known species of butterflies exist on earth, and approximately 800 of these occur in North America. Some 170 to 180 species have been found in the Pacific Northwest, the region covered in this book. Someone who is energetic and experienced might spot half that number in one year by undertaking multiple expeditions in the region throughout the spring and summer. The other species are either scarce, confined to a small area, or seen only when they occasionally stray from their breeding bases in other areas.

A BUTTERFLY'S BODY AND HOW IT FUNCTIONS

Anatomy

Shortly after emerging from its pupa, the Oregon Swallowtail in the picture below is waiting for its wings to harden. The butterfly's body has three main segments: head, thorax, and abdomen. Attached to the head is a pair of prominent, dark, protuberant eyes covered by hundreds or thousands of individual lenses. Each lens transmits light to its own photoreceptors, which have nerve connections to the brain. Together, a lens and its photoreceptors are called an ommatidium. Each ommatidium functions as an independent visual unit, sending its own stream of messages to the brain. Presumably the brain creates a visual image from this information, an image with far less resolution than in human vision. Butterflies' eyes are probably better at detecting motion than at forming a clear, detailed image. They perceive color—even in the ultraviolet range invisible to us.

Two antennae stick out from the top of the butterfly's head; these are equipped with receptors for touch and for identifying different chemical substances. The mouth, or proboscis, of an adult butterfly is a flexible, hollow tube kept tightly coiled and tucked under the head. Part of the coil is visible in the picture of the Oregon Swallowtail. The tube can be straightened and extended to reach nectar within flowers or to suck plant sap, decaying organic matter, or water that contains minerals.

Underside of an Oregon Swallowtail

WILLIAM NEILL

The thorax is the locomotive center, providing attachments for the four wings, the six legs, and the muscles that move these appendages. Five of the Oregon Swallowtail's six legs are showing in the picture on page 3. The legs are long, slender, and jointed. The swallowtail is in a hanging posture, the foot hooks providing a firm grip on the twig. Tiny muscles located within the thorax and within the legs themselves can flex or extend the joints.

We can see the underside of the wings: one entire hindwing, and the tip of a forewing. The wings are thin but stiff enough to support the butterfly's weight when airborne. Struts, called veins, reinforce the wings; in this swallowtail, the veins are black. Tiny, overlapping scales cover the wings in rows, similar to the shingles on the roof of a house. At this magnification, you can appreciate individual scales within the blue area of the hindwing, where blue and black scales are mixed. The flight muscles, within the thorax, move the wings indirectly by distorting the thoracic exoskeleton to which the wings are fastened. The attachment of the wings to the body is delicate, allowing free movement in more than one plane but making the wings vulnerable to accidental separation from the body.

The butterfly's abdomen houses the renal, digestive, and reproductive systems. The swallowtail pictured is a male, and his abdomen ends with a pair of triangular plates, or claspers, used to grasp and stabilize the female's abdomen during copulation.

The butterfly's entire body is covered by fine yellow "hairs"—actually, modified scales called setae. Underneath the setae, the tough exoskeleton encloses and protects the soft internal structures. The exoskeleton consists of a mesh of chitin fibers—chemically more similar to wood than bone—embedded in a protein matrix. The chitin reinforces the matrix like steel bars in concrete. The exoskeleton is rigid over the head and thorax and more flexible over the abdomen.

Internal Fluid Circulation and Breathing

In butterflies, the internal organs are surrounded by fluid. Known as hemolymph, it functions somewhat like blood, delivering nutrients and hormones. The hemolymph circulates throughout the body, propelled by rhythmic contractions of a muscular vessel that runs longitudinally through the abdomen and thorax. The hemolymph enters this tubular heart through openings near the heart's rear (posterior) end. As the muscular tube contracts, valves within it direct the compressed hemolymph toward the head. The hemolymph squirts from the front (anterior) end of the tube, enters the free liquid space within the body, percolates past the living cells, and finally reenters the pores at the rear end of the heart.

In insects, breathing is carried out independently from the internal fluid circulation. A network of tubes carries fresh air directly to the cells, terminating in fine branches in all parts of the body. The tubes open to the outside through a series of pores along the sides of the body, mostly in the abdomen. Butterflies and caterpillars do not breathe through their mouths as we do, and they will drown if their abdomens are kept under water.

It's interesting to compare this breathing arrangement with our own. Vertebrates, including humans, evolved a single strategy for transporting both liquid and gas within the body. The heart pumps blood through a network of closed tubes that branch into microscopic capillaries to reach the cells. The same blood passes through the lungs, where it comes into contact with fresh air, picking up oxygen and discarding carbon dioxide. This design for rapid transport of vital materials over distance has allowed the evolution of huge vertebrate animals, such as dinosaurs, elephants, and whales. The design for butterflies and other arthropods has served them well, judging by their evolutionary success, but it is less capable of transporting oxygen and other substances over long distances and thus limits their possible size. Lobsters and horseshoe crabs are about as big as arthropods have become.

Temperature Regulation

Insects are cold blooded—the temperature inside them varies according to the temperature around them. Butterfly muscles work best when their temperature is about 80 to 100 degrees Fahrenheit. When it is cooler than that, butterflies move less quickly and are an easier target as potential meals. Therefore, butterflies keep out of sight when cold. The temperature in many climates is below 80 degrees much of the time, so butterflies wouldn't have much chance for survival. To get around this problem, butterflies raise their body temperature by absorbing radiant energy from the sun. This is called basking.

When basking, butterflies orient themselves to the sunshine in a manner that maximizes radiant heat absorption. The wings, with their large surface areas, act as heat collectors. Basking butterflies hold their wings in one of two positions: out flat to each side of the body in a horizontal plane (dorsal basking), or clasped together over the back so that the sun strikes the underside of the wings (ventral basking). In either case, the surface of the wing facing the sun is held perpendicular to the sun's rays. Heat gathered by the wings is conducted to the thorax and muscles, where it matters the most. Dark surfaces absorb heat best. Alpine and subarctic butterflies—those with the greatest temperature challenge—tend to have fuzzier, darker bodies, as well as darker coloring of the adjacent portions of their wings, enhancing heat absorption.

Butterflies often choose warm, cozy niches for basking—places with their own microclimate, such as sunny cups of foliage with still air or dark stones that have been in the sun for a while. Basking allows the temperature of thoracic muscles to rise as much as 10 to 15 degrees Fahrenheit above the ambient temperature—often a crucial difference.

Once butterflies begin to fly, their working muscles contribute heat. To maintain warm thoracic muscles while flying through cool air, butterflies must juggle factors of continued absorption of solar energy, muscle metabolism, and the heat that moving air carries away from the surface of the body.

WHAT BUTTERFLIES EAT

The most important food for adult butterflies of most species is nectar, which contains a high concentration of sugar. Many types of flowers—both those native to an area and those that are not—are suitable sources of nectar. Butterflies favor flowers that produce the most nectar. Small butterflies go to small flowers, in which there is only a short distance to the nectar. A butterfly with a short proboscis can't reach the nectar in long, tubular flowers. Different species use nectar to varying degrees. Fritillaries often visit flowers for nectar, whereas many of the browns seem to spend much less time at flowers.

Flowers are not the only source of food for butterflies. Many are attracted to rotting fruit, plant sap, animal carcasses, and feces, especially the droppings of carnivorous animals. I see butterflies on dog or coyote scat, for example, passing up far more plentiful horse droppings along the same trail. The butterflies that I often notice dining at these nonnectar meals are the anglewings, tortoiseshells, admirals, ladies, blues, and crescents. What

A Mourning Cloak, Satyr Anglewing, and Red Admiral share sap oozing from a tree in Wisconsin.

WILLIAM NEILL

nourishment are they extracting? These materials are probably good sources of amino acids, fats, and minerals. Even in small quantities, these substances could be important dietary supplements to nectar, which is essentially carbohydrate in water. Logistically, it's a simple matter for a butterfly to take nectar through its proboscis, because it's liquid. To ingest dry materials, a butterfly first ejects liquid through its tube onto the dry stuff and then sucks up the soup of dissolved nutrients.

Butterflies are often seen with their proboscises inserted into mud. At this time they are also apt to crowd tightly together at one spot. Sometimes the crowd centers on a bird dropping or stained patch of mud; other times there's no obvious reason why one site is especially coveted. Butterflies at mud are virtually always males. Why would only males go for mud, and why would they all light in the same spot? They must be after more than water; this phenomenon likely has something to do with the male's role in reproduction. They are probably mining for minerals or organic nutrients dissolved in the water. These useful materials will be incorporated into the spermatophore that the male leaves with his mate during copulation (see "Reproduction" ahead). In the end, this gift contributes toward the survival of his offspring.

REPRODUCTION

Continuity of Life through DNA

As with other animals, the bodies of butterflies wear out. The species continues because the mortal bodies are temporary carriers of durable genes: complex DNA molecules that are the blueprint for a new body similar to the old one. DNA molecules are not passed on intact, however. Offspring receive DNA from both parents—in an ovum from the mother and in sperm from the father. Each ovum receives a different mixture of the mother's maternal and paternal DNA molecules (grandparents of the offspring). Likewise, each sperm receives a different mixture of the father's maternal and paternal DNA molecules. Moreover, the molecules themselves fragment and reassemble into new molecules as the ova and sperm are formed. Each individual, therefore, is endowed with a unique set of DNA molecules and will be slightly different from its parents and siblings.

Of course, this molecular explanation of how butterflies copy themselves only happens if a male and female, two small animals out in all that space, find and recognize each other, and then physically join together so their genes can combine.

Finding a Mate

In finding a partner, the male butterfly takes the initiative. In some species, he flies back and forth repetitively over the same route, looking for a mate. The route he patrols might be a 100-yard path joining two meadows. Swallowtails, whites, and sulphurs are some of the species that employ patrolling as a mating tactic. Other butterflies, such as anglewings, admirals, hairstreaks, and skippers, more often locate females by perching. The male claims a vantage point—for example, a bush or the relic of last autumn's aster still sticking up at the edge of the field—where he waits for a prospect to fly by. He darts from his perch to investigate practically anything that moves within his sight: another butterfly, a bird, or a person. If a rival male enters the scene, the resident male defends his position by attempting to drive away the intruder, sometimes chasing him skyward in a spiral path and then returning to his original lookout.

Courtship

Potential mates probably recognize each other first by visual clues, relying on color patterns. If the female is on the ground, the male lands next to her. A female in flight may either land, voluntarily or forced down by the male, or else avoid the male and fly away. Once the pair is on the ground close together, they emit chemicals called pheromones that stimulate mating receptivity. The male curls his abdomen to position it against the tip of hers. A female often cooperates at once, or she may flutter away a short distance and be pursued by the male. Repetitive short flights and pursuits can occur. Females can avoid copulation by fluttering their wings and averting their abdomen. An unreceptive female ultimately flies up and away.

As a final precaution against mating mistakes, many species possess unique genital structures that fit together in copulation like lock and key. They don't fit with other species, even closely related ones.

Field Notes

RECOGNIZING HIS MATE

A pair of Silver-bordered Fritillaries were enclosed in a pint jar carpeted by violet leaves on which I hoped the female butterfly would lay eggs. The male was there as insurance, in case the female was virgin the day I captured her. I had been watching them closely. The male and female moved about within their limited space, crawling over the violet leaves and each other. No eggs were laid, nor were the butterflies seen to copulate.

At the end of three days I gave up on the project and released the captives in my yard. The female took flight, heading straight for a dandelion blossom. The male trailed after and alighted on top of her just as she reached the flower. They copulated with a minimum of preliminary fuss, remaining coupled for about twenty minutes.

Evidently, mating was stimulated when the male saw the female in flight. Contact in the jar, no matter how prolonged and intimate, did not suffice.

Copulation

During copulation, the male transfers a spermatophore, a capsule containing millions of sperm plus nutrient materials, to the female. To achieve this, he inserts his aedeagus—the male reproductive organ in insects—into the female through a mating opening at the end of her abdomen near the exit pore of the oviduct. Once in the female, the spermatophore moves through a tube to a storage chamber. Another tube connects this chamber to the oviduct, allowing the sperm later access to the eggs. Copulation usually occurs soon after the female emerges from her pupa, when the eggs in her ovaries are not yet mature. A few days later, mature eggs, singly or in bunches (depending on the species), descend the oviduct, where they pass the waiting sperm and are fertilized prior to their exit from the female's body.

The male and female remain coupled for several minutes to an hour or longer. It's a perilous time, for they are not so agile while joined together. For this reason, they usually seek cover in vegetation, although they can fly and are sometimes seen traveling or feeding at flowers while attached.

Often a female mates only once, rejecting overtures from males that present themselves later. A single spermatophore contains plenty of sperm to fertilize all her eggs. Not all females, however, confine themselves so strictly. Some copulate again and acquire a second spermatophore. A subsequent suitor may appear to offer preferable genes; the female also stands to gain additional nutrients from a second spermatophore. If she does mate a second time, the first suitor may be out of luck, as his spermatophore may have been shoved to a position where access to eggs descending the oviduct is blocked by the second spermatophore.

Parenting

Having contributed his spermatophore, the male has fulfilled his parental role, and he flies away. For the female, searching for the proper host plant and laying eggs dominate her activities for as long as she lives, usually a matter of days. Females of most species place their eggs one at a time. Others—for example, crescents, checkerspots, and the Mourning Cloak—deposit one or more clusters of dozens or even hundreds of eggs each. The female is meticulous about where she deposits her eggs. She examines many sites on a host plant before she parts with an egg. Why she chooses one site and rejects another is largely unknown; possible reasons include better sun exposure to ensure warmth for the growing embryo, the quality of foliage, or more protection from predators. This is her one chance to make choices that might give her offspring an edge in survival. Once the egg leaves her body, the female departs the scene, and the new generation receives no further care from either parent.

Interaction between female and male is limited to the brief period of courtship and copulation. They make no attempt to forge the bond that is so

Stages of Metamorphosis

Anise Swallowtail egg on desert parsley

Young caterpillar, one or two weeks old

Fully grown caterpillar, four or five weeks old

Caterpillar preparing to form a pupa

Fully developed pupa, the next day

Same pupa, the following spring

important among mammals and birds, which share in the nurturing of their young over a long period of time. Limited parental care frees up resources that can be used to produce a very large number of eggs. Only a small percentage of these eggs need to survive to ensure a stable population.

LIFE CYCLE

Metamorphosis: Growth and Maturation

The development of a butterfly—the transition from egg to full-sized adult—proceeds through several distinct phases, each with its own physical form. This process is known as metamorphosis, which means "change of form." A sequence of changes in body form may seem like a tortuous path to adulthood, but as a strategy, metamorphosis has its advantages. Growth from a single cell into a complex adult organism is broken down into separate steps. The different physical configurations of egg, caterpillar, pupa, and adult efficiently accomplish what needs to be done—the butterfly's goal, and ultimately that of the species—at each step.

Form 1: Egg

A butterfly egg is about a millimeter in diameter, about the size of a pinhead. At the outset, it consists of the following three elements: a single microscopic cell endowed with the genetic blueprint for all the details of a marvelous butterfly, a relatively huge store of yolk, or food, and a tough shell that isolates the egg's contents from its surroundings. Usually the egg's surface is intricately sculptured. The shell keeps the egg from drying out but at the same time is gas permeable, allowing the living cells to "breathe." A tiny pore called a micropyle provides entrance for sperm.

The goal during the egg stage is to transform the single gene-containing cell into a functional organism capable of foraging on its own by the time the food provided within the egg by the mother is exhausted. The original cell grows and divides repeatedly, using the stored food to form a mass of cells—the beginning of an embryo. If we could witness this, we would see a vaguely animal form begin to arise from the amorphous yolk material. In only a few days, a complex creature is created that moves about at will and performs purposeful actions. In the overall process of butterfly replication, one of the most remarkable steps takes place within the egg.

Form 2: Caterpillar (Larva)

The infant caterpillar, or mature embryo, chews its way through the eggshell and crawls out into the open. Its first meal is the empty eggshell. The caterpillar is equipped with mandibles for chewing leaves and a large digestive tract. There are three pairs of jointed legs near the anterior end of the body and several primitive prolegs to the rear (see photo of Ochre Ringlet caterpillar, page 155). Together, these stubby appendages provide a sturdy grip and enough mobility to move from one foraging site to the next. Caterpillars have

WILLIAM NEILL

Newborn caterpillar of Great Arctic eating its empty eggshell

no functional eyes, only basic light receptors. The survival strategy of caterpillars centers on not being noticed.

The objective at this stage is to convert plant substance into body mass. The caterpillar's growth is prodigious, amounting to more than a hundredfold increase in bulk in a period of a few weeks, all without significant change in form or function. No growth occurs in subsequent stages, including the adult.

The caterpillar's exoskeleton does not grow and must be replaced periodically to accommodate such rapid enlargement of the body. To do this, the surface layer separates partially from an inner layer of actively multiplying cells. These cells form a new, larger exoskeleton underneath the old, with the new layer temporarily wrinkled upon itself. At this point, the caterpillar expands by engulfing air, and the old exoskeleton splits away completely and is sloughed aside. The underlying layer is now free to unwrinkle and harden. The caterpillar immediately appears larger, but the enlargement is mainly air. The subsequent growth of body tissue displaces the air. A caterpillar molts in this way four or five times, depending on the species. The successive stages of the caterpillar as it grows and matures between molts are called instars; for example, *second instar* describes a caterpillar after its first molt.

Fully grown, the caterpillar finally stops eating and begins to wander. It locates a secluded place, and, in many species, attaches itself by silk strands to something rigid: a stiff stem, woody twig, or overhanging rock. The suspended caterpillar stops moving, usually ejects excess fluid, and shrinks. In two or three days, it sheds its outer covering to reveal a compact pupa.

Molting Anise Swallowtail caterpillar slithers out from its old "skin."

This checkerspot caterpillar located a hidden rock crevice, attached itself by silk to the overhang, and is suspended head down as its first step in pupation.

Form 3: Pupa (Chrysalis)

The pupa is nearly motionless, does not eat, and has essentially no interaction with its surroundings. If provoked vigorously, it may respond by thrashing from side to side. The protoplasm amassed by the caterpillar is now broken down into simpler chemical materials and used to construct the body parts of the adult butterfly. This is accomplished in as little as two weeks. The drama inside takes place without any noticeable change in the outward appearance of the pupa. If you watch, nothing seems to be happening. In the final few days, however, the color and pattern of the adult's wings gradually become visible through the pupa's transparent covering.

Form 4: Adult

The long delicate legs, antennae, and wings of the butterfly are folded and compressed together within the pupal shell. The fully developed adult splits its pupal shell along fault lines and begins to push itself out. As soon as it is free of its pupa, the butterfly scrambles to some nearby perch (often the pupal case itself) from which it can let its wings hang down and straighten. The wings are soft and pliant only for a brief period. Body fluid is forced into the hollow veins of the wings to help the wings expand completely. The wings begin to stiffen within minutes and are ready for use in an hour or so.

The life goal of the adult male butterfly is to locate a mate. The female's life goal is to disperse her eggs. The adult butterfly's mobility is well matched to each role. Its first flight is tentative and comparatively awkward, but that's about as long as it takes the butterfly to learn to use its new wings.

 *Field Notes*

AN UNSOLVED COLD CASE

A Viceroy caterpillar I watched for several days had a habit of sunning on the same small willow twig. On May 3, the caterpillar was at its customary perch. Suddenly, a smaller ladybird beetle entered the field of vision from stage right, coming from the far end of the twig. Advancing nimbly along the narrow twig, this miniature spotted tank looked more comical than threatening, but then I'm not a small soft caterpillar. There was precious little room for passage, and when the beetle came into contact with the caterpillar's rear end, the caterpillar swung its head around aggressively, seeming to threaten the beetle. The beetle scampered past or over the caterpillar—it happened so fast I couldn't follow the details—and exited stage left.

Curiously, the caterpillar kept its head thrust back in the same position with which it had confronted the beetle a moment ago. Since the position didn't seem normal, I wondered if the beetle had bitten the caterpillar during their brief encounter. When I returned the following day, the caterpillar was in exactly the same position and quite dead.

SURVIVAL STRATEGIES

Diapause: Escaping the Adverse Season

I know a mountain meadow where I can walk on a summer day and count on being entertained by butterflies rising up from flowers along the path. If I stop to hunt, I'll find prosperous-looking caterpillars feeding on the same familiar plants. In the winter, that mountain meadow is covered with snow, and I won't see any butterflies. At another place, in a desert where wildflowers cover the sandy ground in May, the resident checkerspots and whites flit about among the flowers. By July, warmth has turned to heat, the flowers have dried up, and the butterflies are gone.

Most butterflies are provincial. They and their progeny live out their entire lives in one place, so they need to be prepared to survive whatever hardships that place presents. When summer ends, only a few of our Northwest species, most notably the Monarch, migrate to escape the coming cold winter season. All the rest remain at their home base or not far from it throughout the year. When conditions turn inhospitable, they enter a dormant state called diapause, in which they can ride out temporary difficulties.

In diapause, physical activity ceases, and metabolism gears down to a level just sufficient to sustain life. This half-sleep state occurs in different stages of metamorphosis in different butterfly species, and progression of the life cycle beyond that stage comes to a halt. By conserving energy, the butterfly can

A migrating Monarch in Illinois has found a surviving remnant of original tallgrass prairie. This piece of broken ground, too rocky to be farmed, now serves as a haven for wildlife within a sterile sea of cornfields.

stay alive in this condition for many months without food, or even for a few years as a pupa.

So when you walk across a mountain meadow in winter, its summer butterflies are all there, but you can't see them. The anglewing that flew among the asters last October has slipped from sight into a fissure in the bark of that Douglas fir, where it grabs hold and waits and waits. Eggs fastened to twigs won't hatch until spring. Tiny, young fritillary caterpillars have crawled into the ground litter, now deeply blanketed by snow, where they sleep until violets begin to grow again. Swallowtail pupae have postponed their transformation into adults, suspended until the change in seasons starts the necessary hormonal sequence back in motion.

Sometimes a single individual initiates diapause. For example, a caterpillar may become dormant if its food supply dries up before it is fully grown. In most cases, though, diapause is a routine part of the life cycle. For example, the caterpillars of the Anicia Checkerspot butterfly that inhabit the Alvord Desert grow for a brief period in the spring, then diapause until the fresh Indian paintbrush leaves that they use for food reappear the following year. That's a long time to fast. However, in this species, diapause has become a regular part of the life cycle, occurring even in unusually wet years when the paintbrush plants offer satisfactory foliage into the summer.

The progression of metamorphosis is integrated with the seasons of the year. The timing differs between species—for example, some species hibernate as an egg, other species as an adult, and so forth. All members of a given species, however, adhere to the same plan. Adults emerge at about the same time so they can fly together and find mates. Caterpillars emerge when they can expect fresh vegetation. If you discover caterpillars, you're not likely to also see adults of that species in the same place on the same day. Conversely, if adults are flying, chances are you won't find their caterpillars.

Some butterflies have one brood per year, others have two broods, and a few have three. At the other extreme, arctic or alpine butterfly species can take more than one year to complete their life cycle. Among butterflies with two annual broods, diapausing during the winter interrupts the progression of one brood, but not the other. In the first brood of the Anise Swallowtail, the pupae form in early summer and develop into adults in two to three weeks. Pupae of the second brood form at the end of summer and enter diapause until the following spring. Some signal related to the season—daylight length, temperature, or change in the foliage the caterpillar is eating—apparently initiates diapause in the second brood.

Some individuals will vary from the routine, perhaps as a kind of insurance against extinction. In a species that produces two broods annually, there is the unusual individual of the first brood who deviates from its siblings and enters diapause, thus avoiding any potential environmental disaster to which the majority of its generation may be exposed. As another example, some pupae continue diapause for years, sidestepping the consequences of hatching during a prolonged drought with no host plants on which adults could lay their eggs. Diapause for multiple years is especially common among species in desert regions.

Predation, High Reproductive Capacity, and Population Gyrations

How long does a butterfly live? The answer varies radically depending on whether you're referring to the entire life, from the time the egg leaves its mother, or only to that portion spent as an adult. The entire life, from egg through adulthood, is one year for butterflies that produce one brood annually. If there are two broods, the life span is shorter—a few months for the summer brood and longer for the brood that hibernates. Life as an adult butterfly is shorter—typically no more than a few weeks in the warm seasons, or several months for those that hibernate as adults.

These numbers represent maximum life spans, which seldom are achieved. Average actual lives are much shorter because most butterflies meet premature deaths. In all stages of development, butterflies are victims of freezing, drowning, starvation, infection, and predation.

To start with, ants and other small insects and spiders eat butterfly eggs and young caterpillars. Larger caterpillars and pupae are preyed upon not

A crab spider hiding on a vetch blossom ambushes a butterfly that came for a sip.

WILLIAM NEILL

Aerial assassination of Ridings' Satyr. The ferocious robber fly seized its prey in mid-flight, drove it to the ground, and pierced the butterfly's thorax with its proboscis.

DOUG HEPBURN

only by ants, hornets, ambush bugs, and spiders, but also by lizards, birds, and mice. Many parasitic flies and wasps infest caterpillars with their own eggs. Larvae hatching from these eggs burrow into the hapless caterpillar to feed on its body, growing at the expense of the host, which ultimately dies.

As they land to feed, adult butterflies are ambushed by white or yellow crab spiders and by insects, all ready to grab the butterfly and pierce its body to suck its internal juice. Toads, lizards, mice, and birds pounce on adults as they roost at night and on rainy days. Butterflies are trapped in spider webs. I've seen them snatched from the air by dragonflies, robber flies, and birds.

In most cases, ants treat caterpillars mercilessly as prey, but not in all. Some of the blues and hairstreaks have evolved a remarkable symbiotic relationship with ants. When the ants stroke them on the back with their antennae, the caterpillars of these butterflies secrete, from glands on their backs, a sweet treat that the ants eagerly imbibe (see photo on page 19). It is likely that caterpillars receive compensation beyond being spared. Ants have a reputation as very tough customers within their miniature world. Their mere presence near the caterpillar might be a menacing deterrent to would-be predators. The results of field experiments do suggest that caterpillars tended by ants survive better than the same kind of caterpillars without ants.

Obviously, despite these perils, butterflies manage to carry on from one generation to the next. Those few that reach maturity produce a lot of eggs, sometimes hundreds. The ability to produce a large number of eggs or offspring, referred to as high reproductive capacity, can make up for

A Melissa Blue caterpillar tended by ants

WILLIAM NEILL

heavy subsequent losses. Also, rapid growth and short life cycles reduce their exposure to daily casualties, making it more likely that an individual will reach the finish line at the end of the gauntlet.

Some simple calculations produce a quantitative appreciation of the amount of predation and other types of premature death affecting butterflies. Assume that one in three individuals survives each of the four stages of the life cycle—egg, caterpillar, pupa, and adult. How many starter eggs are necessary to produce a pair of reproductive parents? The answer is about 170 eggs (170 x $\frac{1}{3}$ x $\frac{1}{3}$ x $\frac{1}{3}$ x $\frac{1}{3}$ = 2). Theoretically, 170 eggs would offset a mortality rate of two out of three at each stage, yielding a stable population. Now see what would happen if survival at each stage improved to two out of three. Using the same math, those 170 eggs would yield 34 reproductive adults—a population jump of seventeenfold in one generation.

Animals with high reproductive capacities tend to experience rapid swings in population from one extreme to the other. When environmental conditions for survival are ideal—for example, food is plentiful or competitors and enemies are few—their numbers soar. When conditions are unfavorable, the population crashes. When better times return, recovery can be swift. Butterfly populations vary quite a bit from one year to the next. The numbers of some, such as the Painted Lady and California Tortoiseshell, vary more than those of others.

FOOD CHAIN—FOLIAGE, GRAZER, PREDATOR

Something fell from above. It made a faint whining buzz on the way down, then a tiny tap as it hit the ground. I crouched down. A yellow jacket astride a struggling, much bigger caterpillar was biting the caterpillar behind its head. In less than a minute, dark greenish liquid began oozing from the wound. The yellow jacket continued to work with its sharp mandibles, and in another two or three minutes had carved a manageable piece from the middle of the caterpillar. The yellow jacket lifted off with this parcel, circled over the dying caterpillar, then flew in a straight line to the west, presumably headed for its nest.

The yellow jacket returned shortly, circled the site, and landed next to the caterpillar. It repeated the sequence of carving portions from its prey, flying off loaded, and returning for more about twenty times, transporting the entire caterpillar in about 90 minutes. With each trip, the yellow jacket circled the area coming and going and was always a bit uncertain in relocating the caterpillar. Its imprecision improved neither with repetition nor when I placed a bright orange plastic cup adjacent to the caterpillar as a potential additional bearing. There was never more than one yellow jacket on the scene, and the timing between trips did not change. Apparently, one yellow jacket did the whole job.

Adaptability

In discussing reproduction, I've emphasized that each individual butterfly is genetically unique. With high reproductive capacity, each new generation steps forth as a huge group of competitive young butterflies presenting a spectrum of different genetic characteristics. When the environment changes, there is a good chance that one or more of these genetic variations will be ready to capitalize on the situation. Those individuals best equipped to cope with the new conditions will be more likely to survive and, in turn, reproduce. The composition of the new population will shift to one better suited to the changed environment.

BUTTERFLIES AND PLANTS

Symbiosis: Nectar Traded for Cross-fertilization

Butterflies are one of many types of insects that serve as vectors or carriers in the cross-fertilization of flowering plants. As a butterfly probes a flower to obtain nectar as food, its legs and body incidentally pick up pollen, the male element needed to fertilize a plant's ovum. Later, when the butterfly moves to another flower, some of the pollen brushes off on the flower's stigma, whence it can reach the plant's ovum, or seed, for fertilization. This mutually beneficial relationship between butterflies and plants is an example of symbiosis, a word that means "living together," particularly in reference to dissimilar organisms or species.

A plant benefits in this exchange only if the butterfly visits another flower of the same species; the plant achieves nothing by having its pollen deposited on some other kind of flower. It's important to remember here that animal behavior is subject to habit. A butterfly that has just received a good nectar meal at one blossom looks for another like it. Observe butterflies feeding in a field of mixed flowers. A butterfly will tend to favor a single species—say, a white daisy—and move directly from one daisy blossom to the next. Eventually,

Field Notes

A STUCK PROBOSCIS

It was hot in the Klamath River canyon on June 24, 2002. At first sight, the Silvery Blue dangling lifelessly from a dogbane flower (*below*) suggested ambush by a crab spider, a scene familiar enough to me. In this case, though, there was no predator. The tip of the butterfly's proboscis was simply lodged in the flower's nectary alongside the style. I could imagine the butterfly's pitiful struggle, trying in vain to get free, because twenty years previously I had witnessed such a struggle—a fritillary beating its wings furiously while suspended in air at the side of a showy milkweed flower. The butterfly's proboscis was stuck. While I was contemplating the most effective heroic method of assistance, the butterfly freed itself.

Butterflies use dogbane and milkweed frequently. The nectaries of both flowers are guarded by narrow tubular entrances, which apparently—though rarely—snare a proboscis.

Silvery blue caught in dogbane

DOUG HEPBURN

this pattern is broken—the butterfly stops visiting daisies—but it repeats the pattern with a different kind of flower, perhaps a yellow groundsel this time. The unique shapes and colors of flowers apparently evolved so pollinating insects could distinguish plants in the same field. An impression similar to "That tasted good. Where's another?" induces the insect to deliver its burden of pollen to a flower of the same species. The perfect flower provides a measured level of satisfaction to its insect diners. Too little nectar would fail to attract customers, but if the butterfly's appetite were fully satiated, it would not be motivated to move on to the next blossom.

Host Plants

Nectar is nice but, for the welfare of butterflies, plants are even more important as a source of food for caterpillars. As plants had their foliage eaten by caterpillars and other animals, they evolved ways to defend themselves. These defenses include physical characteristics such as hardness, spines, and hairs, which make it more difficult for caterpillars to bite off pieces or digest them. Other defenses are chemical: compounds in foliage that inhibit intestinal absorption or toxins that kill the caterpillar if it succeeds in digesting the foliage.

Caterpillars answered the plants' challenges by evolving countermeasures of their own: enzymes to penetrate hard coatings or dissolve hairs, antidotes to toxins, and altered metabolic pathways to bypass chemical poisons. Caterpillars today tend to be highly specialized foragers limited to a few related food plants they can safely use as food. This outcome suggests that it has been more efficient for them to develop countermeasures narrowly focused on foiling one type of plant defense rather than many types.

The plants a caterpillar uses are referred to as its host plants, a term that accurately describes who in the relationship is providing the banquet and who is the guest. Unlike with the butterfly and the flower, the relationship between the caterpillar and the host plant is not mutually beneficial; the caterpillar gains at the plant's expense. Some caterpillars, for example the Oregon Swallowtail and the Hoary Elfin, accept only one host plant as food. Others, such as the Painted Lady and Gray Hairstreak, have a broader range of host plants. Often, if a caterpillar eats food other than its host plants, it will become sick or die. Given the strict menu limitations of its caterpillar, a butterfly species can only colonize places where its host plants grow.

In the larger scheme of things, caterpillars help control the native plants with which they have evolved. Alien plants that invade this territory often lack similar restraints and proliferate, becoming troublesome weeds.

COLOR: HOW AND WHY

The scales covering the upper and lower surfaces of a butterfly's wings are responsible for their color. Rub away the scales, and you'll see that the membranous wings underneath are transparent. The colors come mainly from pigment, although in some butterflies, shades of blue and purple also are affected by the physical structure of the wing scales. Scales that have a grooved surface refract light and cause iridescence, changing hue or brilliance with the angle of light. The spots on the underside of fritillaries are brilliant silver from one angle and dull bluish gray from another. The angle of light determines the brilliance as well as the hue of the tops of blue butterflies. This iridescent effect is especially pronounced in the Silvery Blue and the Greenish Blue. Among the coppers, the direction of light exerts varied effects. The tops of the Purplish Copper and the Lilac-bordered Copper change from dull brown to shiny purple, whereas in the Ruddy Copper and Lustrous Copper, the sparkle comes and goes, but the red color stays the same.

Why should butterflies bother with clothing themselves in extravagant patterns of color? Two likely reasons are mate recognition and protection against predators. To find a mate, a butterfly must be able to recognize another member of its species. Visual clues are more obvious if the members of a species are conspicuously different from other species. The more distinctive their decorations, the easier it is for potential mates to identify each other.

Color patterns give a tactical edge in avoiding predators in several ways, not only for the adult butterflies but for their caterpillars as well. Here are some examples of what's known as protective coloration, categorized by strategy:

Camouflage. Many butterflies blend with their background by taking on its general color tone or by looking like something in the surroundings, such as a piece of bark or a leaf (see Hoary Comma adult, page 134, and the caterpillar of Johnson's Hairstreak, page 91).

Startle. Bright, bold patterns would seem likely to attract too much attention, but they can startle a predator when, disturbed, a butterfly breaks cover and flashes its wings. A split-second delay can be all the butterfly needs to make its escape (see Two-tailed Swallowtail adult, page 46).

Decoy. Bright markings on the hindwings of many species of hairstreaks seem designed to attract attention to the periphery of the wing and even to look like the head of the butterfly (see Gray Hairstreak adult, page 86). A bird or lizard attacks this point, expecting to strike a fatal blow, but only tears away a bit of wing It's common to see this portion of the hindwing torn off on these butterflies—evidence of a foiled predator attack.

Warn. Poisonous caterpillars and adult butterflies are flamboyantly marked so predators can learn to recognize them beforehand and avoid them (see Monarch, page 140).

Mimic. If they aren't actually dangerous themselves, many butterflies and caterpillars copy a creature that is. Some mimic another, unrelated poisonous butterfly. If unable to distinguish the mimic from the real thing, predators avoid both (see Viceroy, page 143). Others have eyespots that look like the eyes of a snake or owl (see Common Buckeye, page 153).

Observing Butterflies in the Pacific Northwest

FINDING AND WATCHING BUTTERFLIES

In the broad meadow where I stopped to rest, morning is getting on by the time the sun clears the tops of the trees behind me. I look across to the opposite edge of the meadow, where it is hemmed in by a wall of forest, and watch the morning light march down the sides of the trees. Now the warm light is chasing shadows across the meadow, melting away the dew, unveiling patches of wildflowers. Here come the butterflies, roused from their sleep in the deep grass and tangled

Field Notes

HUNKERING DOWN

We get to know butterflies by watching what they do out in the open when the sun shines. But what do they do at night or when it rains?

On June 6, clouds were gathering for an evening storm. The low sun broke through on and off, illuminating the west side of a little hill. A few Silver-bordered Fritillaries still on the wing at 6 p.m. began to congregate there, where the sun warmed them. Two settled together on a clover stem, wings folded together over their backs. A couple of hours later, the rain was still holding off, but the sun was gone for the day. The butterflies were in the same place, still exposed. One stretched her wings slowly back and forth for a few strokes, then folded back up.

It drizzled during the night, and the next day stayed dark and showery. I didn't return to the field until the end of the day. The two butterflies had moved a few inches, and their forewings were pulled down closer to their bodies, perhaps to shrink their profile. One had stepped to the underside of a large clover leaf and clung there upside down.

The third day started with weather much the same. After a final shower, at 2 p.m., the sun glared through convincingly. I hurried back and found my subjects on the same plant, sunning themselves, wings spread, moving about. They flew directly to clover blossoms, one promptly after the other, taking nectar avidly, as if they were restless and hungry after being holed up for the past forty-eight hours.

brush. Butterflies soaring, skimming, fluttering over the flowers. The lemony sulphurs are hogging the show, but it's the little Northern Blue that I came to see this morning.

Look for butterflies in the warm sunshine. You'll find them on flowers, drinking on moist ground, or on a rock or patch of bare ground that's been toasted by the sun. Find an old field, one that's been ignored by farmers and ranchers long enough to harbor a mixture of native plants. That's where butterflies find the host plants their caterpillars need to eat. Host plants are almost always part of the indigenous flora, not the crops and ornamentals planted by humans. Most butterflies don't stray far from the food they eat as caterpillars. The greater the variety of native plants, the more kinds of butterflies you'll see.

For their own food, adult butterflies visit many kinds of flowers, native and alien. They favor the flowers that produce the most nectar. Blue, purple, or white flowers seem to attract more butterflies than red, orange, or yellow ones. Small butterflies generally go to small flowers, ones with nectaries that can be reached by a short proboscis. Although some composite flowers look big at a glance (like thistle or rabbitbrush), their individual flowers may be in scale with blues, hairstreaks, and other small butterflies.

More than a hundred Eastern Tiger Swallowtails congregate on an old dirt road in a New Hampshire wood.

WILLIAM NEILL

In the countryside, seek out dogbane, horsemint, thistle, and milkweed. It's best if the flowers are in the sun. If you don't see butterflies around these flowers, move on to another site. Chances are, there aren't many butterflies in the neighborhood.

After flowers, the most irresistible lure for butterflies is mud. A natural stream that trickles across or along a dirt road or path—one that just dampens the earth—is ideal. Or look for a seep wetting a rock face exposed to the sunshine. Sometimes there are crowds of butterflies, all males, and they may even bunch tightly together in a knot. (For speculation on male butterflies, crowding, and mud, see page 7.) You will also find butterflies on rotting fruit, an animal carcass, feces (especially of carnivores), or sap oozing from a tree trunk.

Sunshine, flowers, and varied native plants are the three main elements of good butterfly habitat. So, where in the Pacific Northwest do you find this combination? You might try any of these:

• The open pine forests east of the crest of the Cascade Mountains, such as along the western tributaries of the Deschutes River or in the Wenatchee Mountains.

• Riversides in the canyons of Oregon's high desert and the Columbia Basin—for example, along the John Day, Owyhee, and Okanogan Rivers.

• The alpine ridges and montane meadows of Mount Rainier, Mount Adams, Steens Mountain, the North Cascades, the Wallowa Mountains, and the Siskiyou Mountains.

• Neglected, weedy roadsides wherever you find them.

Butterflies follow the seasons. They're most abundant in the spring and early summer at low elevations—for example, in the Columbia, Deschutes, and Illinois River canyons—and in mid- to late summer in high places like Mount Rainier, the North Cascades, and the Wallowa Mountains.

Don't expect a rich assortment of butterflies in densely farmed regions. While the fertile low prairies in western Oregon and Washington must have supported butterflies in abundance at one time, and isolated remnants of these areas still do, crops disagreeable to caterpillars have replaced the original flora. The variety of butterflies in and around our population centers is also disappointing. Why? Mainly because most caterpillars don't share our enthusiasm for concrete and exotic trees and shrubs.

Butterflies are small, so satisfactory observation means getting close. Since they are wary and intent on avoiding attention, sneaking up on them successfully calls on tact and patience. Here are some ways to improve your chances:

• If the butterfly is flying, don't chase it. The compound eyes of insects efficiently detect movement within their broad field of vision. Alarmed, the butterfly will keep moving farther away.

- Approach a butterfly when its attention is focused on something else. If it seems interested in a flower, hang back until it lands on the flower and begins to probe for nectar.

- Approach slowly in a line directly toward the butterfly, keeping as low a profile as possible.

- Blend your outline with a nearby shrub. Don't cast a moving shadow directly on a butterfly—if you do, you're finished!—or anywhere the butterfly can see it.

- Tread softly. Butterflies probably can't hear you talk, but they can detect vibrations through their legs, especially if they are on the ground.

- A butterfly drinking water from mud often remains in one place for several minutes—ideal for photographing. You may succeed in crawling within inches, provided you proceed stealthily.

- When a pair of butterflies is in the process of courting, give them space. Be patient until they have joined in copulation. Once attached, they're not likely to separate and are inclined to stay put.

Magnification is a good substitute for moving closer without spooking the subject. Using binoculars with near-focus, you can stand back 10 or 20 feet from a stationary butterfly and see it well enough to identify it and watch it without distracting it. Even when you're photographing butterflies using a macro lens, the magnification may help you notice some interesting behavior as you work on the focus or composition of the picture. Of course, the final picture helps you correctly identify the butterfly you were watching.

An Edith's Checkerspot drinks sweat from a child's hand.

GEOGRAPHY AND HABITATS

In this book, Pacific Northwest refers to a biological zone encompassing the states of Washington and Oregon and the touching edges of Canada, Idaho, Nevada, and California. This region as a whole has a reputation for rain and forest. Some of it is indeed wet forest, but most is not. The warm moist air that flows inland from the Pacific Ocean loses much of its moisture in the form of rain or snow as the air climbs up and over the high, cool Cascade Mountains. Beyond this formidable barrier, arid conditions prevail. Other mountains obstruct and redirect the airflow, creating a patchwork of local climates with their own flora and fauna. The conditions for butterfly colonization differ greatly from one area to the next. The following outline describes some major features of these terrains—including human impacts—as they influence butterfly distribution.

Coast Range

A chain of mountains anchored at its northern end by the Olympic Mountains and at its southern end by the Siskiyou Mountains.

Olympic Mountains
  Highest peak: 9,000 feet
  Description: Very wet on the west side, drier rain-shadow areas on the east side; conifer forest, subalpine meadows
  Butterfly habitats: Subalpine meadows, streamsides
  Butterfly variety and density: Medium
  Examples of species: Arctic Blue, Northern Blue, Arctic Fritillary

Siskiyou Mountains
  Highest peak: 7,000 feet
  Description: Varied local climates, some dry; open, mixed conifer and deciduous forest; intrusion by California flora and fauna, for example, the Gray Marble
  Butterfly habitats: Streamsides, roadsides, other forest openings
  Butterfly variety and density: High
  Examples of species: Gorgon Copper, Great Copper, Leanira Checkerspot, California Sister

Central Coast Range
  Highest peak: 4,000 feet
  Description: Wet; mostly second-growth forest and dense brush
  Butterfly habitats: Streamsides, roadsides
  Butterfly variety and density: Low
  Examples of species: Margined White, Satyr Anglewing, Hydaspe Fritillary

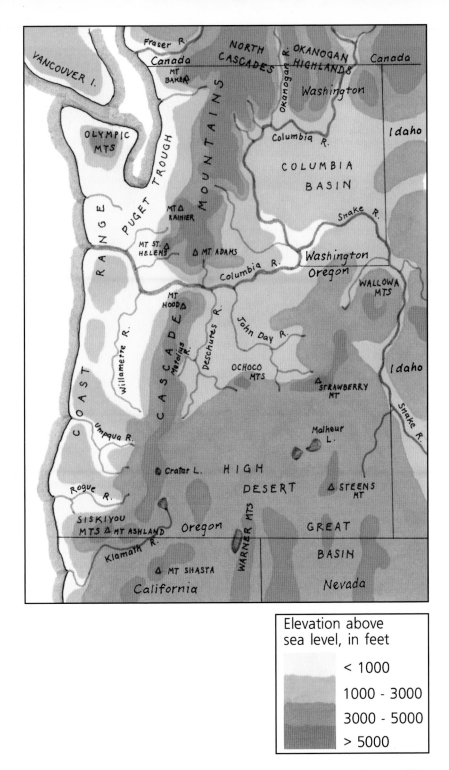

Coast Range foothills, elevation 1,000 feet, in June. Flowers and host plants grow along a road through the forest.

Willamette Valley in May. A rough field alongside a farm provides a limited breeding space for butterflies.

Willamette Valley Lowlands and Puget Trough
Description: Flat and wet; habitats very disturbed by urbanization and farming
Butterfly habitats: Edges of woods, neglected fields
Butterfly variety and density: Low
Examples of species: Silvery Blue, Cabbage White, Purplish Copper, Sara's Orangetip

Cascade Mountains
Glaciated mountains with peaks reaching 10,000–14,000 feet. North Cascades portion intruded by fauna based mainly in contiguous Canadian mountains; for example, Astarte Fritillary.

Western Slope
Description: 1,000–4,000 feet; wet; dense fir and hemlock forest with broadleaf evergreen understory
Butterfly habitats: Forest meadows
Butterfly variety and density: Low in forests, medium in meadows
Examples of species: Western Meadow Fritillary, Spring Azure, Clodius Parnassian, Johnson's Hairstreak

Western slope of the Cascades, elevation 3,000 feet, in June. This moist, sunny meadow surrounded by conifer forest is suitable habitat for several species of blues and fritillaries.

DOUG HEPBURN

Rock outcrop on an alpine ridge in the North Cascades, elevation 7,000 feet, in July. Ground-hugging plants include heather, saxifrage, lewisia, and sedum. Habitat for Astarte Fritillary and Arctic Blue.

Cascade Crest
Description: 4,000–7,000 feet; subalpine conifer forest; montane and subalpine meadows; ridges
Butterfly habitats: Montane and subalpine meadows, rocky ridges
Butterfly variety and density: Medium, with fewer butterflies at higher elevations
Examples of species: Hoary Comma, Western White, Mariposa Copper

Eastern Slope
Description: 2,500–5,000 feet; progressively drier eastward; open pine forest with mixed shrubs, grasses, and flowers under trees
Butterfly habitats: Open forests, meadows, streamsides, roadsides
Butterfly variety and density: High
Examples of species: Western Pine Elfin, Cedar Hairstreak, Lorquin's Admiral, Great Arctic

Columbia Basin, High Desert, Great Basin
Description: 2,000–5,000 feet; flat or rolling arid prairie, mostly treeless. Columbia Basin: Native flora largely replaced by agricultural crops, especially grains. High Desert: Sagebrush prairie, livestock grazing. Great

High Desert, elevation 4,000 feet, in May. Drought-tolerant grass, buckwheat, and yarrow grow amid the sagebrush.

The Owyhee River canyon in southeastern Oregon, elevation 3,000 feet, in May. Plant growth and butterfly populations peak this month in the warm canyons of the high desert.

Basin: Extends far into Nevada and Utah; sagebrush prairie, livestock grazing; meager rainfall that gathers in sinks and evaporates.
Butterfly habitats: Canyons, hills
Butterfly variety and density: Locally high in canyons, low on prairie
Examples of species: Spring White, Ruddy Copper, Two-tailed Swallowtail, Great Basin Wood Nymph

Eastern Mountains

Okanogan Highlands
Description: 6,000–8,000 feet; an eastward extension of the North Cascades; rolling meadows and rounded mountaintops; sparse trees
Butterfly habitats: Meadows, mountaintops
Butterfly variety and density: High
Examples of species: Blue Copper, Mormon Fritillary, Chryxus Arctic, Common Alpine

Okanogan Highlands, elevation 6,000 feet, in July. Broad meadows with potentilla, paintbrush, lupine, aster, and arnica alternate with patches of conifers. Trees become sparser farther east.

WILLIAM NEILL

Wallowa Mountains

Description: Steep granite mountains up to 9,000 feet; forested; high lake basins, subalpine meadows, alpine ridges; floral and faunal extensions (for example, Pelidne Sulphur) from the Rocky Mountains via mountains in Idaho across Hell's Canyon of the Snake River

Butterfly habitats: Subalpine meadows, ridges, streamsides

Butterfly variety and density: Medium

Examples of species: Mountain Parnassian, Mariposa Copper, Mormon Fritillary, Milbert's Tortoiseshell

Ochoco Mountains

Description: 4,000–6,000 feet; rolling hills and rounded mountains; open pine forest with plentiful grasses and flowers growing underneath

Butterfly habitats: Meadows

Butterfly variety and density: High

Examples of species: Western Sulphur, Callippe Fritillary, Great Spangled Fritillary, Dark Wood Nymph

Ochoco Mountains, elevation 4,000 feet, in June; meadows with varied grasses, flowers, and woody plants growing in sunlit ponderosa pine forest

DOUG HEPBURN

Top of Steens Mountain, elevation 9,000 feet, in July, with low-lying alpine plants. Vestiges of snow persist in depressions until late summer.

The eastern escarpment of Steens Mountain meets the Alvord Desert at 4,000 feet elevation. Photo taken in May. Paintbrush, balsamroot, penstemon, daisies, and many other plants bloom for a short period in the spring.

Steens Mountain
  Description: The west side is a prairie starting at 4,000 feet that slopes up to a ridge at 9,000 feet; the east side is a steep, 5,000-foot escarpment. Isolated stands of aspen trees.
  Butterfly habitats: High meadows, alpine ridges
  Butterfly variety and density: High
  Examples of species: Queen Alexandra's Sulphur, Lustrous Copper, Shasta Blue, Zerene Fritillary

Observing Butterflies at Home

A BUTTERFLY GARDEN WITH CATERPILLARS

More and more people are considering butterflies when they plan their gardens. At first, this simply meant choosing flowers that promised to attract the most butterflies. As the public's understanding of butterflies has become more sophisticated, the approach has broadened to include the needs of the other phases of the butterfly's life cycle as well.

Flowers providing lots of nectar will bring butterflies to our gardens, where we can watch and enjoy them. That has merit for us, but has it significantly benefited the butterflies? Not unless nectar was in short supply to start with. That could be, in some cases, but residential areas are usually rich in flowers and poor in caterpillar host plants. Most of our landscaping—unhappily, even many of our butterfly gardens—can't support the life cycles of our resident butterflies. It is the absence of caterpillar host plants that is threatening the existence of our neighborhood butterflies.

In your garden, include flowers that butterflies especially like for nectar, such as bee balm, lavender, cosmos, aster, and zinnia. The flowers can be aliens if you wish. Put in enough different kinds to ensure that something will be blooming throughout the warm season. Now for the important part, the one that we tend to neglect: be sure to place host plants nearby so female butterflies will notice them as they visit your flowers. If they do, there is a good chance they'll lay eggs. Around Portland and Seattle, try planting thistle for Painted Lady and Mylitta Crescent, currant and nettle for anglewings and Red Admiral, mustard for Sara's Orangetip, and fennel for Anise Swallowtail. Don't expect to lure butterflies that are not already residents of your region. A butterfly that normally lives in the alpine meadows of Mount Hood or Mount Rainier is not likely to visit your garden in Portland or Seattle, even if you do plant appropriate host plants. Find out what butterflies live in your area. Any species that you have actually seen in your neighborhood would be a promising candidate. Use the facts in the Species Accounts in this book, about range, preferred habitat, and host plants of individual species, to help you select likely choices. Then, of course, do not use pesticides. It's not nice to poison the guests you invite to dinner!

The place where you grow the host plants should remain rough. Leave sticks and fallen leaves where they lie. These provide the kinds of settings that butterflies need to hide from predators, lay eggs, and pupate. Rather than throwing out obscure eggs, caterpillars, and pupae along with the yard debris, be prepared to tolerate enough messiness for the butterflies to complete their life cycle. The less you clean up, the better.

When creating a butterfly garden, keep these important components in mind:

• Plant mixed flowers for nectar to bring the adults to where you can enjoy them—and where the females will notice the host plants you have set out for them.

• Plant specific host plants tailored to egg-laying females patrolling the neighborhood.

• Maintain a natural, undisturbed environment year-round for the butterflies' life cycle.

That's what I call a butterfly garden!

REARING BUTTERFLIES

You can watch the life cycle of a butterfly unfold in your own nursery. Rearing butterflies from caterpillars does not require special expertise or equipment. You need only to obtain an egg or caterpillar, provide the caterpillar's specific host plant for food, and exercise a bit of careful routine housekeeping.

Feeding caterpillars is not like tossing table scraps to a pet rabbit. As discussed, each species of butterfly has a specific plant that its caterpillar uses as food. Look for its eggs or caterpillars on that kind of plant. Eggs are firmly attached to the foliage and they won't fall off. If possible, snip off the stem that holds the egg and leaf, and place the cut end in water. This should keep the foliage fresh long enough for the caterpillar's first meal when it hatches. If you begin with a caterpillar, cage it in a roomy glass jar—a pint or quart jar will suffice. Cover the opening with cloth or netting to allow ventilation. Too much ventilation dries and withers the leaves, while too little ventilation promotes mildew. Place a small amount of the host plant's leaves in the jar. Usually, the caterpillar will refuse to eat any substitute or will die if it does. Keep the jar dry, cool, and out of the sun. Empty the jar's refuse daily and replenish it with fresh leaves from the plant. Caterpillar feces are dry pellets that fall out cleanly.

An alternative arrangement is to place a stem or twig of the host plant into a bottle or vase filled with water. That way the foliage will stay in better condition, although there are some potential problems with this setup. You'll need to be willing to tolerate the dry droppings that your pet will shower around the vase. The caterpillars usually stay up on the leaves, but sometimes they crawl down the stem into the water and drown. You can control this by using a narrow-necked vessel with tissue stuffed around the plant's stem. Don't forget, caterpillars routinely wander from the host plant just before pupation, so you need to anticipate when this is going to happen. That's not easy unless you've raised similar species before.

The caterpillar will change to a pupa in a few weeks. Just before it does, it stops eating, often wanders about, and may take on a sickly appearance. Don't give up hope; it is not about to die. It may eject some messy liquid, so absorbent paper at the bottom of the jar or base of the vase is useful. The caterpillars of many butterflies attach themselves by silk threads to something firm. Confined, the caterpillar is apt to suspend itself attach to the side of the jar or the cloth cover. A small twig propped up within the jar provides an alternative site and makes for easier handling of the pupa later. Once the caterpillar fixes itself in position, allow it to form a pupa without disturbing it.

The pupa itself requires no special care. It may hatch in a few weeks. Other species hibernate in this form and hatch the following spring. You can keep the jar outside over the winter—for example, a porch that is out of the rain and protected from predators is a suitable place. If the pupa is kept in a warm house, it will probably hatch prematurely, before spring.

You can also obtain eggs from an adult female butterfly, although they are not always cooperative. Enclose the butterfly together with its host plant. A paper grocery bag or cardboard box will do. If you keep an adult captive for longer than a day, you should feed it. Soak tissue in sugar water or diluted honey, then hold the butterfly by its wings so its feet touch the tissue. Often, it's necessary to uncoil its proboscis with a toothpick to initiate feeding.

If you accidentally discover an unknown caterpillar, it could be either a moth or a butterfly. A moth is more likely, since they are much more common. No single characteristic separates moth caterpillars from those of butterflies, but in general, hairless "loopers" (inchworms) and very soft, fuzzy caterpillars will turn out to be moths. Why be disappointed with a moth? Chances are, it will be just as interesting and beautiful. Many kinds of parasitic wasps and flies lay their eggs on caterpillars, leaving no clues of their visit. If your caterpillar was infected by the time you found it, one or more of these parasites may emerge from the pupa instead of the anticipated butterfly. Look at this as part of the adventure. In rearing butterflies, the uncertainty adds excitement.

ETHICS OF CAPTURING BUTTERFLIES

I'd like to comment about the ethical issues of catching butterflies, keeping them captive, or killing them in order to study or display them as specimens. Usually, butterflies caught in nets made of suitably soft material are not injured, but accidents occasionally do occur. Legs or wings can be broken, especially if the butterfly is caught in flight. You can significantly reduce the chance of injuring a butterfly if you wait until it stops at a flower or settles on the ground. To catch a stationary butterfly, lower the rim of the net over the butterfly while holding the end of the net bag up with the other hand so that the butterfly flies up into the end of the net, not down under the rim. If your net bag is not deep enough for this to work, get one that is.

To hold a butterfly, it's safest to grasp it by its wings. Using your forefinger and thumb, gently press its wings together behind its back. It doesn't hurt it if you rub off a few wing scales. If you enclose a butterfly in a jar even for a short time, keep it out of the sun. The inside can heat up quickly enough to kill its inhabitant in a few minutes. As long as a closed jar is kept cool, it holds plenty of oxygen for a butterfly for a considerable period of time.

Some people make collections of butterfly specimens, which entails killing them. Under almost all circumstances, taking sample specimens has no significant impact on the population, nor does it pose a risk to the species. The exception is when intense, repeated collecting occurs in a population restricted to a small area, such as an isolated bog or mountaintop. Collectors have a responsibility to recognize and limit collecting in these vulnerable situations. In addition, collectors need to know which species are protected under the Endangered Species Act and therefore are not to be collected. At present, two Pacific Northwest butterflies are federally listed and thus off-limits: Fender's Blue (page 101, top right) and Oregon Silverspot (page 115, top right).

Aside from the importance of protecting certain unique populations and species, there is the question of the morality of taking the life of any individual animal. I don't have an answer that I would attempt to impose on others. My opinion is that each of us should formulate a personal code of ethical behavior and then be personally responsible for it. When I collect butterflies, I am restrained by the belief that every life has value. Every time I put a butterfly in my sights, I demand an answer to the question: Do I want to keep this butterfly as a specimen strongly enough to take away its life?

Conservation

The explosion of human population, its prosperity, and its consumption of natural resources is staggering the world's ecology—including impacts on butterfly populations. At present, it doesn't seem possible to stop human expansion, so let's focus on the most important factors threatening butterflies and realistic steps we can take on a smaller scale in our own neighborhoods.

Our contamination of the planet with toxic chemicals—incidental byproducts of our various endeavors—is harmful to all animals, including butterflies. Moreover, we unintentionally kill a lot of butterflies when we attempt to eliminate or control insects that we consider pests. Pesticides invariably poison a broad range of insects. Even the microbial agent Bt, which many people think infects only gypsy moths, infects and kills the caterpillars of all butterflies and moths. Once butterfly and moth populations have been decimated by Bt, the absence of caterpillars in the region can then starve the insects, birds, and other animals that depend on caterpillars as food.

While the chemical and bacteriological onslaught is tough on butterflies, our most significant impact on them is in shrinking and degrading the habitats in which they reproduce and live. Whether through urban spread, agricultural expansion, inadvertent introduction of invasive weeds, or simply tidying up rough areas within our view, habitat available to them is squeezed into a smaller and smaller space. Marshes and bogs are drained, and then sprayed crops, lawns, or asphalt replace the native host plants that butterflies used for food. Prairies are grazed and left to sagebrush or else irrigated and planted with cultivated grains. Mixed forests are cut and "reforested" with tight rows of Douglas fir. Suburbs eat up fields and woods. Humans are forever cutting, digging, plowing, mining, irrigating, paving, and planting. We seem bent on replacing natural diversity with an order of our own making.

We aren't likely to return many farms to native prairies, but perhaps we can manage some of the margins—streamsides, hedgerows, roadsides—in a way that is more friendly to butterflies, not to mention other native flora and fauna. The wide, sunny strips along freeways have great potential. Since they are often covered with a monoculture of some alien plant, we could try convincing the highway department to use indigenous plants instead, many of which are attractive, hardy host plants for butterflies.

Our northwest forests are crisscrossed by dirt roads, built to provide access. These roads can be an asset to butterflies: the corridors let in sunlight, and various flowers and shrubs grow along the edges of the roads. Butterflies colonize these new roadside habitats that, left alone, are usually dominated by native plants. Eventually, forest saplings invade, and the strip is sprayed with herbicides or all the vegetation is cut to ground level. The life cycle of the resident butterflies is interrupted and their population crashes. These man-made corridors would provide better butterfly habitats if the management style controlled encroaching forest without eliminating other native vegetation.

Large public landscape projects—parks, schoolyards, cemeteries, golf courses—are planted with grass and imported shrubs. Could we set aside small portions of them for native plants?

For the foreseeable future, we seem destined to work within a background of increasing pressure on limited natural resources—most importantly, the land. With such a heavy headwind, we may have to get used to accepting fixes that slow the pace of further losses as a substitute for gains. We need new ideas, compromises that balance economic efficiency with habitat diversity. Those who earn their living from agriculture, for example, will be more receptive to setting aside space for insect habitat if they see collateral benefits from pollination of their crops.

SPECIES ACCOUNTS

A written description and one or more photographs follow for each of these 118 species. Gender is specified for butterflies in photos when known. The descriptions are structured as shown below, with the following information:

Name (Common name)   *Name* (Scientific name)
A.k.a., (Also known as; alternative common and scientific names)

Wingspan: The distance between the tips of the forewings when positioned as below in diagram.

Description: Field marks and other significant physical features of the species. Descriptions apply to both males and females unless gender is specified.

Range in PNW: Geographic distribution of the species within the Pacific Northwest. Based on recorded field observations, including those compiled by John Hinchliff in *The Distribution of the Butterflies of Oregon* and *The Distribution of the Butterflies of Washington.*

Habitat: Environment in which the species is typically found.

Host plants: Common and scientific names of plants most frequently used for food by the species' caterpillar.

The diagram below orients you to descriptive terms used in the species accounts.

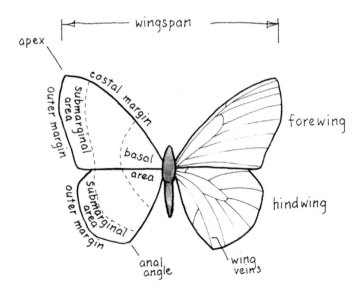

SWALLOWTAILS

Western Tiger Swallowtail *Papilio rutulus*

Wingspan: 3⅛–3½ inches

Description: The **top** is yellow with black vertical stripes and black wing borders. The hindwing has a tail, a red spot at the anal angle, and submarginal blue crescents (more prominent in females).

Range in PNW: Throughout

Habitat: Forest openings and streamsides

Host plants: Deciduous trees, including bigleaf maple (*Acer macrophyllum*) and species of aspen and cottonwood (both *Populus*) and willow (*Salix*)

The big yellow butterfly that swoops into your backyard is likely a Western Tiger Swallowtail. Members of this species survive well amidst our homes because many of the trees we allow to grow around us can be used by their caterpillars as food. The butterfly's bold vertical stripes are tigerlike. In the male Western Tiger shown here, the red and blue spots are mostly hidden where the hindwings overlap below the body. The full-grown green caterpillar, adorned with a pair of false eyespots, has fastened a network of silk fibers over the surface of the cottonwood leaf for a more secure footing. The egg is similar to that of the Pale Swallowtail. Western Tiger Swallowtails produce one brood, with adults emerging in early summer.

DOUG HEPBURN

WILLIAM NEILL

Pale Swallowtail *Papilio eurymedon*

Wingspan: 2⅞–3¼ inches

Description: The **top** is creamy white with black vertical stripes and broad black wing borders. The hindwing has a tail, a red spot at the anal angle, and submarginal blue crescents.

Range in PNW: Throughout, except in treeless prairies

Habitat: Forests and mountains

Host plants: Species of *Ceanothus*, red alder (*Alnus rubra*)

Like the Western Tiger Swallowtail, the Pale Swallowtail's black stripes run parallel to the body. This male had been taking nectar from columbine blossoms and stopped to rest on a serviceberry bush overhanging the Metolius River. The June morning was cool and still. Later it became hot and the air smelled of pine resin. That's when you find groups of pale swallowtails on the mud at the side of the river. Immature stages are shown on the facing page. Spherical eggs resembling green pearls are glued to ceanothus leaves, usually on the upper surface. Caterpillars emerge in a little more than a week. At first they are black with a white saddle, but as they grow, green invades and ultimately replaces the black, as seen in the picture of a partially developed caterpillar shown here. When fully grown, the caterpillar is 1¾ inches long and has narrow false eyespots and a row of blue dots along each side of its body. It looks much like the Western Tiger Swallowtail caterpillar. As a youngster, the caterpillar spends most of its time among the foliage. Larger caterpillars, when not eating, tend to move toward the center of the bush to rest on stems. Just before pupation, when the caterpillar leaves its host plant and travels over the ground, its color turns to brown. Pupae can be either green or brown. Pale Swallowtails produce one brood a year.

DOUG HEPBURN

WILLIAM NEILL

WILLIAM NEILL

WILLIAM NEILL

Two-tailed Swallowtail   *Papilio multicaudata*

Wingspan: 3⅜–3⅞ inches

Description: The **top** is yellow with black vertical stripes and black wing borders. Each hindwing has two tails, a red spot at the anal angle, and submarginal blue crescents.

Range in PNW: East of Cascade Crest and in Siskiyou Mountains

Habitat: Canyons and riversides

Host plants: Chokecherry (*Prunus virginiana*)

Bigger than the other swallowtails, the Two-tailed Swallowtail has more yellow and has an extra tail on each side. The symmetrical nicks on the outer margin of both forewings of the female shown here are the signature of a bird's beak, presumably inflicted when the butterfly's wings were clapped together in an evasive maneuver—which evidently succeeded. All swallowtail caterpillars in the Pacific Northwest are dark with a light saddle when young. The one shown here is about half grown. We took its picture just after prodding it with a twig in order to demonstrate the forked pink appendage, or osmeterium, which the caterpillar extrudes from a slit behind its head. The osmeterium emits a pungent, sweet odor meant to deter predators. Other swallowtail caterpillars are armed with the same smelly instrument.

DOUG HEPBURN

WILLIAM NEILL

Oregon Swallowtail *Papilio oregonius*

A.k.a., Baird's Swallowtail, Old World Swallowtail, *P. bairdii, P. machaon*

Wingspan: 2⅛–2⅜ inches

Description: The **top** is yellow with black outer margins, a black basal area of the forewing, and black patches along the costal margin. The hindwing has a tail, a red spot at the anal angle that contains an eccentric black pupil, and submarginal blue crescents.

Range in PNW: Columbia and Snake River basins (east of The Dalles) into Idaho

Habitat: Arid canyons

Host plants: Tarragon (*Artemisia dracunculus*)

The Oregon Swallowtail is similar to the Anise Swallowtail but usually is bigger and has more yellow. Moreover, the black pupil in the red spot is located at the edge of the spot. This is Oregon's official state butterfly. The adult male in the picture has just hatched from its pupal shell, which is still attached to the stem above it. Look for the gorgeous caterpillars on tarragon growing in side canyons of the Columbia Gorge. Go to these canyons in May or June for the first brood of caterpillars and, if you can stand the heat, return in August for the second brood. The mature caterpillar shown here is almost two inches long.

Anise Swallowtail   *Papilio zelicaon*

Wingspan: 2½–2¾ inches

Description: The **top** is yellow with black outer margins, a black basal area on the forewing. and black patches along the costal margin. The hindwing has a tail, a red spot with a centered black pupil at the anal angle, and submarginal blue crescents.

Range in PNW: Throughout

Habitat: Many, including mountaintops and urban areas

Host plants: Parsley family, especially *Lomatium grayi*; fennel (*Foeniculum*); and others

The Anise Swallowtail looks much like the Oregon Swallowtail, except it is smaller and darker and its black pupil is positioned at the center of the red eyespot on the hindwing. The two males in the picture are sucking moisture from the ground where an old mining road crosses Pine Creek in the Elkhorn Mountains of eastern Oregon. The immature stages of the Anise Swallowtail are shown on page 10. The caterpillars seem quite adjusted to fennel, an alien herb that is cultivated in some gardens and grows abundantly in disturbed, weedy lots. A friend in Portland discovered six mature caterpillars on a large fennel plant in her garden.

DOUG HEPBURN

Indra Swallowtail   *Papilio indra*

Wingspan: 2¼–2½ inches

Description: The **top** is black with a pale yellow band and spots. The hindwing has a short tail, a red spot with a central black pupil at the anal angle, and submarginal blue crescents.

Range in PNW: Steens, Siskiyou, and Wallowa Mountains and eastern slope of Cascade Mountains

Habitat: Canyons and mountain ridges

Host plants: Species of desert parsley (*Lomatium*), including *L. grayi*

Indra is our only swallowtail that is mostly black and has tails that are no more than meager stubs. Indra Swallowtails fly early, in some places together with Anise Swallowtails. Males visit flowers and mud, but I've never seen large numbers of them at one time as with other swallowtails. The females are seen much less frequently; presumably they spend their time looking for parsley plants in less accessible areas. Indra Swallowtails have only one brood per year. Initially the caterpillars are dark with a pale saddle, but they soon change to velvety black with yellow bands.

PARNASSIANS

Clodius Parnassian   *Parnassius clodius*

Wingspan: 2¼–2½ inches

Description: The **top** is pearly white. The forewing has dark gray bars at the costal margin and its outer half is gray and transparent. Only the hindwing has red spots. The antennae are solid black.

Range in PNW: Cascade Mountains westward and Wallowa Mountains

Habitat: Edges of moist forests

Host plants: Species of bleeding heart (*Dicentra*), including *D. formosa*

Where white scales are absent, the wings are transparent and appear gray. During copulation, the male parnassian deposits a soft white material at the end of his partner's abdomen, which hardens and prevents further mating but does not hinder the passage of eggs. This structure, called a sphragis, is plainly visible beneath the abdomen of mated females. Clodius Parnassians lay eggs in August. The stems and leaves of the host plant, bleeding heart, wither and disintegrate in the winter, so females attach eggs to more durable nearby structures. Emerging the following spring, the caterpillars have a short trek to the bleeding heart foliage. The caterpillars are velvety black with bright yellow spots, perhaps designed to simulate a dangerous centipede. The caterpillars pupate on the ground among fallen leaves, using silk to pull leaves and other debris together into a protective nest.

DOUG HEPBURN

WILLIAM NEILL

Mountain Parnassian   *Parnassius smintheus*

A.k.a., Phoebus Parnassian, *P. phoebus*

Wingspan: 2–2½ inches

Description: The **top** is white. In males, the forewing has two black spots along the costal margin, often accompanied by red spots, and the transparent gray area is confined to the submarginal area. In females, the gray area is much more extensive and the black and red spots are more prominent. The hindwing has two red spots. The antennae are banded black and white.

Range in PNW: Siskiyou, Olympic, and Wallowa Mountains, and Washington's Cascade Mountains eastward and northward into Idaho and Canada

Habitat: Sunny rock outcroppings in mountain forests, and exposed mountain ridges

Host plants: Species of stonecrop (*Sedum*)

Compared to the Clodius Parnassian, males of the Mountain Parnassian are more opaquely white and females are darker, but the most reliable difference between the two species is their antennae: solid black in the Clodius, black and white in the Mountain. The male (left) and female (right) shown here are basking in the sun at 7,000 feet in the North Cascades. Their wings are flattened against the warm, lichen-covered rocks. The fuzzy black body and the dark scaling on adjacent parts of the wings trap solar energy to warm the thoracic flight muscles, important in the cool alpine home of this butterfly. I've heard that in the Orient, parnassians are called Red Pearls—a fitting description of their red spots, right down to the white highlights.

WILLIAM NEILL

DOUG HEPBURN

WHITES

Western White *Pieris occidentalis*
A.k.a., *Pontia occidentalis*

Wingspan: 1⅜–1⅝ inches

Description: The **top** is white with black marks on the forewing of males and on all the wings of females. On the **underside** of the hindwing are gray-green stripes along the wing veins, which often are blurred and may taper to points at the outer margins.

Range in PNW: Cascade Mountains eastward

Habitat: Many

Host plants: Mustard family, including *Lepidium*

The markings of the Western White and Spring White are similar. The Western White is one of many species of butterfly that use hilltops and mountain peaks for mating rendezvous. Competing males arrive in midmorning and remain on duty until late in the day. Females (inset), newly emerged, fly uphill, following the contour of the land to the highest point as if familiar with the plan. After mating, the females return to lower elevations to locate appropriate host plants for their eggs.

Spring White *Pieris sisymbrii*

A.k.a., *Pontia sisymbrii*

Wingspan: 1⅜–1⅝ inches

Description: The **top** is white with fine black marks on the forewings of males and on all the wings of females. On the **underside** of the hindwing, the wing veins are overlaid by fine gold lines bordered by distinctly delineated gray-green stripes. These stripes terminate squarely at the outer wing margins.

Range in PNW: East of Cascade Mountains, and Siskiyou Mountains southward into California

Habitat: Arid prairies

Host plants: Mustard family, including *Sisymbrium*

Spring Whites fly among the sagebrush in early spring, even on sunny days in February. They are marked much like Western Whites, but the black markings are generally more delicate in the Spring White. The greenish stripes along the veins on the underside of the hindwing are more distinct in the Spring White. Each of these stripes has a triangular dark segment halfway to the outer edge of the wing. If you squint, the sum of these dark segments forms a curved band arcing across the center of the hindwing. A male is pictured on the left.

WILLIAM NEILL

WILLIAM NEILL

Cabbage White   *Pieris rapae*

Wingspan: 1½–1⅝ inches

Description: The **top** is white, dingy in females. The forewing is dusted with black at the apex and has black spots, usually one in males and two in females. The **underside** is cream or pale olive.

Range in PNW: Throughout

Habitat: Many

Host plants: Cabbage and broccoli (*Brassica oleracea*) and species of nasturtium (*Tropaeolum*)

The white butterfly you see flitting about your garden is almost certain to be the Cabbage White. A European butterfly, it was inadvertently introduced to this continent in the nineteenth century. Lacking natural restraints in its new environment and already adapted to some of our garden plants, the species steadily expanded over most of North America. The Cabbage White seems to be at home around intensely developed urban regions where few other butterflies prosper. Look for its spindle-shaped pale yellow eggs on the underside of cabbage, broccoli, and nasturtium leaves. The caterpillars are green with a fine yellow line on the sides and grow a little more than 1 inch long. The Cabbage White's life cycle repeats two or three times a year, and adults are around from early spring into fall. A female is shown at top left.

DOUG HEPBURN

WILLIAM NEILL

WILLIAM NEILL

Margined White   *Pieris marginalis*

A.k.a., Mustard White, Veined White, *P. napi*

Wingspan: 1½–1⅝ inches

Description: The **top** is creamy white and unmarked. The **underside** of the hindwing is yellowish, and the veins are outlined by a subdued brown, at least in the spring brood.

Range in PNW: Throughout, except treeless prairies

Habitat: Forest openings

Host plants: Mustard family, including *Dentaria* and *Rorippa*

The spring brood has stripes along the wing veins on the underside, as in our photo; in the summer brood, the stripes are attenuated or absent. This is a native North American butterfly that apparently was once common across the northern United States. Settlers largely replaced the indigenous mustard plants used by the Margined White with cultivated alien varieties to which the Cabbage White had long been accustomed in Europe. Both species are attracted to the cultivated mustards and lay eggs on them, but Cabbage White caterpillars grow healthy on this food while the native Margined White caterpillars often do not survive. As a result, the European invader has taken over vast open regions of the continent while its native relative has retreated to woodsy fringes less affected by humans.

DOUG HEPBURN

Becker's White   *Pieris beckerii*

A.k.a., *Pontia beckerii*

Wingspan: 1⅜–1⅝ inches

Description: The **top** is white with brown or black marks on the forewing of males and on all the wings of females. There is an intense black square at the costal margin of the forewing, especially in desert populations. The **underside** of the hindwing has broad olive bands along the veins, interrupted by a curved central white patch.

Range in PNW: East of Cascade Mountains

Habitat: Arid canyons, prairies, and deserts

Host plants: Mustard family, including *Sisymbrium* and *Schoenocrambe*

The field mark that best distinguishes Becker's White from the Western White is the interruption of the olive green stripes on the underside of the hindwing. Females attach their eggs to the leaves, stems, and flower petals of mustard plants. Their eggs are yellow and spindle-shaped with longitudinal grooves. The caterpillars, which have bands of yellow alternating with black dots, eat all parts of the plant. Like ably wielded scythes, their mandibles "cut the mustard," fibrous stems and all. The Becker's White has two broods per year.

WILLIAM NEILL

WILLIAM NEILL

Pine White   *Neophasia menapia*

Wingspan: 1½–1¾ inches

Description: The body is thin and delicate. The **top** is parchment white, and the forewing has a black costal margin and apex. The wing veins on the **underside** are outlined in black, more prominently so in females. The hindwing of females has red edges.

Range in PNW: Throughout, except treeless prairies

Habitat: Conifer forests

Host plants: Pine trees (*Pinus*), including ponderosa, white, and lodgepole, and Douglas-fir (*Pseudotsuga menziesii*)

With its slender body, thin papery wings, and hesitant flight, a Pine White is a butterfly with a delicate demeanor. Flying high among conifer trees, they could be mistaken for drifting pieces of paper. Adults are on the wing late in the season, in August and September. A female is pictured on the right, a male on the left. Eggs attached in rows along conifer needles overwinter. The green caterpillars eat the needles the following spring and summer and pupate in the trees.

WILLIAM NEILL

WILLIAM NEILL

Sara's Orangetip   *Anthocharis sara*

Wingspan: 1 ⅛–1 ½ inches

Description: The **top** is white in males and pale yellow in females. Both genders have an orange patch near the forewing apex. The **underside** has fine gray-green marbling.

Range in PNW: Throughout

Habitat: Many

Host plants: Mustard family, including *Sisymbrium* and *Arabis*

Sara's Orangetip is our region's only white butterfly with bold, orange-red wing patches easily visible in flight. The species is one of the earliest butterflies to emerge in the spring. On April 10, I watched a female pause at a delicate desert mustard plant in the Deschutes River canyon. She left the spindle-shaped orange egg (top right) attached by its tip to a stem. A pale longitudinal stripe on the mature green caterpillar looks like light reflecting from a stem, helping the caterpillar blend in with the plant. The pupa, formed in May, initially is green (bottom left), then fades to a warm neutral color. The faded pupa mimics a spent leaf; to survive, it must remain unnoticed until it hatches in the spring, almost a year later.

DOUG HEPBURN

WILLIAM NEILL

WILLIAM NEILL

WILLIAM NEILL

WILLIAM NEILL

Gray Marble   *Anthocharis lanceolata*

Wingspan: 1½–1¾ inches

Description: The **top** is creamy white, and the forewing has a black spot in the center and black marks at its hooked apex. On the **underside**, the hindwing and the apex of the forewing have brown-gray stippling.

Range in PNW: Southwestern Oregon into California

Habitat: Arid hillsides and canyons

Host plants: Mustard family, including *Arabis*

A hooked forewing silhouette and gray marbling are the key field marks. Mainly a California species, the Gray Marble also appears in the Siskiyou and Warner Mountains of southern Oregon in May and June. When the sun slipped behind a cloud on a cool spring day, the butterfly in the photograph landed on the ground to keep warm. The underside blends with the background of its arid habitat.

WILLIAM NEILL

Large Marble *Euchloe ausonides*
A.k.a., Creamy Marble

Wingspan: 1⅜–1⅝ inches

Description: The **top** is creamy white (golden on some females) with black marks on the forewing apex and costal margin. The **underside** of the hindwing is marbled olive green.

Range in PNW: East of Cascade Mountains, and southwestern Oregon southward into California

Habitat: Prairies, sunlit forests, and montane meadows

Host plants: Mustard family, including *Sisymbrium* and *Arabis*

The Large Marble is similar to the Pearly Marble but is bigger and more yellow. Also, the black mark at the costal margin is narrow and delicate, and the olive green marbling on the underside is sprinkled with white spots. Both marble species employ hilltops as mating sites, but it is the more athletic Large Marble that tears from one side of broad mountain meadows to the other. Momentarily resting, the butterfly shown here is acutely in touch with its surroundings: visually, with its prominent compound eyes; chemically, with its erect antennae; and tactilely, through sensory nerve receptors in the joints and muscles of its legs and feet, ready to detect a stalker that carelessly jiggles the blade of grass.

DOUG HEPBURN

Pearly Marble   *Euchloe hyantis*

A.k.a., California Marble

Wingspan: 1 1/4–1 3/8 inches

Description: The **top** is white with black marks at the forewing apex and costal margin. The **underside** of the hindwing has lime green marbling.

Range in PNW: Siskiyou Mountains southward into California, and arid lands east of Cascade Mountains

Habitat: Canyons, deserts, and hot dry prairies

Host plants: Mustard family, including *Arabis*

Compared with the Large Marble, the white on the Pearly Marble's top is whiter; the marbling on the underside is greener and not sprinkled with white dots. Both marble species have a prominent rectangular mark at the center of the costal margin. This rectangle is wider and more intense in the Pearly Marble. Some lepidopterists consider the western population of this butterfly in the Siskiyou Mountains and the eastern desert population (shown here) to be two separate species. The green caterpillars eat the tiny leaves of rock cress but seem to prefer the flower petals.

WILLIAM NEILL

WILLIAM NEILL

SULPHURS

Clouded Sulphur *Colias philodice*

Wingspan: 1½–2 inches

Description: In males, the **top** is yellow with a solid black border; in females, the top is yellow or greenish white with a black border dotted with white or yellow. The **underside** of the hindwing has a central pearly spot (with a small satellite) encircled by two pink-brown rings. There is a submarginal row of black dots.

Range in PNW: Cascade Mountains eastward, and Siskiyou Mountains southward into California

Habitat: Many

Host plants: Pea family, including *Astragalus, Lupinus,* and *Lathyrus*

The Clouded Sulphur and the Orange Sulphur are the only sulphurs with a large encircled pearly spot and submarginal black dots on the hindwing. Males of the two species can be distinguished from each other by their top surface—yellow or orange. Females that are yellow or orange can also be readily identified. However, I find no way to tell the greenish white females apart. The photograph shows the underside of a male taking nectar from an aster.

WILLIAM NEILL

Orange Sulphur   *Colias eurytheme*

A.k.a., Alfalfa Butterfly

Wingspan: 1¼–2 inches

Description: In males, the **top** is bright orange with a solid black outer border; in females, the top is bright orange or greenish white with a black outer border spotted with orange or white. The **underside** of the hindwing has a large pearly spot (with an adjacent satellite spot) encircled by two pink-brown rings. There is a submarginal row of black dots.

Range in PNW: Throughout

Habitat: Many

Host plants: Pea family, including alfalfa (*Medicago*)

Although the wing patterns of the Clouded Sulphur and the Orange Sulphur are the same, you can tell them apart by their color, except in the white females. In the male shown here, the solid black border on the upper surface of the wings shows through to the underside well enough to easily establish the gender, whereas the orange color of the top is barely perceptible. Resting sulphurs habitually display only their undersides. In flight, however, the orange color is easy to see. Both the Clouded and Orange Sulphur hang out around urban areas and farms, and the Orange Sulphur caterpillar is capable of inflicting some damage to alfalfa fields. Both sulphur species also show up on mountaintops at the end of the summer.

WILLIAM NEILL

Western Sulphur   *Colias occidentalis*

Wingspan: 1¾–1⅞ inches

Description: In males, the **top** is yellow with a black outer border; in females, the top is pale yellow, and the forewing apex is dusted with black scales. The **underside** of the hindwing is golden yellow with a central pearly spot sometimes encircled by a pinkish brown ring. The wing fringes are pink.

Range in PNW: Ochoco, Siskiyou, and Olympic Mountains; east slope of Cascade Mountains; and an isolated colony in southeastern Oregon desert

Habitat: Open forests and meadows

Host plants: Pea family, including *Lupinus* and *Lathyrus*

The four males in the photograph are drinking from mud. The butterfly clinging to foliage is a female. Her underside is pale greenish yellow, and just enough of the upper surface of the opposite forewing shows to reveal the black dusting. In early summer, females attach their spindle-shaped eggs, which are pale green or sometimes orange, to the underside of lupine or wild pea leaves. The caterpillars hatch in one or two weeks, graze for a few weeks, then become inactive in preparation for hibernation. Feeding resumes in the spring. A mature caterpillar and pupa are also shown. Transformation to adult within the pupa is nearly complete, as a yellow wing outlined by pink is visible beneath the pupa shell.

DOUG HEPBURN

WILLIAM NEILL

WILLIAM NEILL

WILLIAM NEILL

Pink-edged Sulphur   *Colias interior*

Wingspan: 1½–1¾ inches

Description: In males, the **top** is yellow with a black outer border; in females, the top is pale yellow with a black outer border on the forewing only. The **underside** of the hindwing is pale yellow with a central pearly spot sometimes encircled by a pink-brown ring. The wing fringes are pink.

Range in PNW: East slope of Cascade Mountains, and northeastern Oregon and Washington eastward into Idaho

Habitat: Forest openings

Host plants: Species of blueberry (*Vaccinium*)

The photos show a male taking nectar in the North Cascades and a female crouched down in a mat of blueberry and kinnikinnick growing under a pine and tamarack canopy. Compared with the Western Sulphur, which it closely resembles, the Pink-edged Sulphur has a paler underside, and the females usually have more black on the tips of the forewings. Also, it flies about two weeks later. This species lacks the black dusting in the basal area of the top surface of the wings that is present to some degree in other sulphur species in the region; however, stationary sulphurs almost never display the upper aspect of their wings.

DOUG HEPBURN

WILLIAM NEILL

Pelidne Sulphur *Colias pelidne*

A.k.a., Skinner's Sulphur

Wingspan: 1⅜–1¾ inches

Description: In males, the **top** is yellow with a black outer border; in females, the top is yellow or white with a black outer border on the forewing, extending variably to the hindwing and invaded at its inner edge in a scalloped pattern by yellow or white. The **underside** is yellow suffused by black scales, especially on the hindwing. The wing fringes are pink.

Range in PNW: Wallowa Mountains eastward into Idaho and an isolated colony on Steens Mountain

Habitat: High mountain meadows near timberline

Host plants: Species of blueberry (*Vaccinium*)

The Pelidne Sulphur resembles the Western Sulphur, but it's smaller and its underside is dusky rather than golden. Females are easier to identify by the distinctive scalloped black border on the upper surface. The pictures here show the underside of a female feeding on nectar, a ribbed, spindle-shaped egg attached to a blueberry leaf, and two caterpillars. The smaller caterpillar, less than half an inch long, is ready to seek cover for a long, frigid winter. It's September at 7,000 feet, and snow will soon blanket the land. Imagine a blowing December night, our caterpillar under the snow—a bit of green life in a vast frozen stillness. Enough of the caterpillars somehow survive. The larger one did, for example, and once the land was cleared of snow and friendly to living things again, it resumed its business of eating blueberry leaves.

WILLIAM NEILL

DOUG HEPBURN

WILLIAM NEILL

WILLIAM NEILL

Queen Alexandra's Sulphur   *Colias alexandra*

Wingspan: 1¾–2 inches

Description: In males, the **top** is yellow with a narrow black outer border; in females, the top is yellow or pale greenish yellow with black dusting on the apex of the forewing. The **underside** of the hindwing is usually gray-green with a small central pearly spot. The apex of the forewing is pointed.

Range in PNW: East of Cascade Mountains

Habitat: Arid prairies

Host plants: Species of *Astragalus*

Most of the time you can recognize Queen Alexandra's Sulphur in the field, even from a distance—which may be as close as you'll get. Queen Alexandra's is bigger than its relatives and more clearly yellow (partly because there is less black), and it frequents a different habitat (arid prairies). Note the straight outer margin and pointed apex of the forewing in the photo below. A strong flier, this sulphur is suited for the wide country where it lives.

DOUG HEPBURN

COPPERS

Lustrous Copper   *Lycaena cuprea*
A.k.a., *L. cupreus*

Wingspan: 1–1⅛ inches

Description: The **top** is an iridescent, fiery red-orange with black spots and black wing borders. The **underside** of the hindwing is gray with black spots and a submarginal crinkled orange line.

Range in PNW: North Cascades northward into Canada, central Oregon southward into California, and mountains of Idaho

Habitat: Mountain meadows

Host plants: Species of dock (*Rumex*), mountain sorrel (*R. paucifolius*), alpine sorrel (*Oxyria digyna*)

No other butterfly in our region looks like this brilliant red and gray gem. The males and females are alike. The Lustrous Copper seeks meadows adjacent to open forest, more often than not mountainous, and it likes to visit flowers. It is not common, but isolated colonies occur in Oregon in the Ochoco, Strawberry, and Steens Mountains; in the Klamath County high prairie; and in the not-so-easily-reached peaks of Washington's North Cascades.

DOUG HEPBURN

Great Copper   *Lycaena xanthoides*

Wingspan: 1⅛–1½ inches

Description: The **top** is gray-brown; in females, it is streaked with dull orange. The hindwing has submarginal orange crescents. The **underside** of the hindwing is pale buff with black-rimmed brown spots and, especially in females, submarginal orange crescents.

Range in PNW: Siskiyou Mountains southward into California

Habitat: Meadows

Host plants: Species of dock (*Rumex*)

Key features of this species are its large size for a copper, its dull upper surface, and its pale, spotted underside. The picture on the left shows a male. The Great Copper and Edith's Copper can be difficult to tell apart. The Great Copper is larger, and the underside is paler and has smaller spots. Apparently this butterfly once occurred in the Willamette Valley, but in recent years it's been found in the Pacific Northwest only in the Siskiyou Mountains. I've seen it in August along Pilot Rock Road east of the freeway at Siskiyou Summit and nectaring on goldenrod at Silver Fork Gap on Mount Ashland.

WILLIAM NEILL

WILLIAM NEILL

Edith's Copper   *Lycaena editha*

Wingspan: 1–1¼ inches

Description: The **top** is gray-brown; in females, it is streaked with dull orange. The hindwing has faint submarginal orange crescents. The **underside** of the hindwing is pale gray-brown with large black-rimmed brown spots and submarginal orange crescents, which are bordered medially by an irregular white band.

Range in PNW: Northeastern Oregon, southeastern corner of Washington, Cascade Mountains in Oregon eastward, and southward into California

Habitat: Mountain meadows

Host plants: Species of *Potentilla* and dock (*Rumex*)

Like the Great Copper, Edith's Copper is a conservative dresser for a copper, and the two are easily mistaken for each other. Edith's Copper is smaller, and the white band on the underside of the hindwing stands out more clearly against the darker background. A common setting for Edith's Copper is a sunny meadow in the forest. The butterfly pictured here was basking in one while the morning was still cool. Its knees are flexed to bring the body down against the warm rock. Note the white band on the hindwing.

DOUG HEPBURN

Ruddy Copper   *Lycaena rubida*

A.k.a., *L. rubidus*

Wingspan: 1 ⅛–1 ¼ inches

Description: In males, the **top** is iridescent fiery red-orange; in females, the top is orange streaked with brown. The **underside** is cream with black spots on the forewing only.

Range in PNW: East of Cascade Mountains

Habitat: Arid prairies

Host plants: Species of dock (*Rumex*)

None of the other coppers can match the fiercely bright red-orange color of the male Ruddy Copper, shown here. Females are more subdued, resembling some of the other coppers on their top side. Visit the lonely high desert region in midsummer to enjoy a glimpse of this butterfly. Drive the highway from John Day up past Seneca to Burns or take the road between Silver Lake and Lakeview, keeping your eye out for a red jewel on goldenrod or a metallic glint across yellow rabbitbrush. Flowers and butterflies are all the more thrilling seen against a stark desert background.

DOUG HEPBURN

Gorgon Copper *Lycaena gorgon*

Wingspan: 1¼–1⅜ inches

Description: The **top** of the male is rusty with a purplish iridescence; the top of the female is yellow-orange and brown. The **underside** of the hindwing is pale buff or yellow with large black spots and submarginal orange crescents.

Range in PNW: Southern Oregon southward into California

Habitat: Arid rocky hillsides

Host plants: Species of buckwheat (*Eriogonum*)

The Gorgon Copper is as big as the Great Copper, but the Gorgon has spots on the underside that are black, not brown with black rims, and the pale area on the top surface of females is a bright yellow-orange color. The Gorgon is mainly a California butterfly whose territory includes the adjacent part of Oregon. I've come across it regularly on the dry hillsides overlooking the Illinois River, in the Siskiyou Mountains southeast of Ashland, and in the deep canyon of the Klamath River. These are hot places during its flight period, June and July. Both genders are fond of taking nectar, especially from buckwheat, which is also the caterpillar's food.

DOUG HEPBURN

Tailed Copper   *Lycaena arota*

Wingspan: 1–1 ⅛ inches

Description: The hindwing has a tail. In males, the **top** is slightly iridescent brownish purple; in females, the top is yellow-orange and brown. The **underside** of the hindwing is warm gray with black spots and squiggles and a submarginal convoluted white band, usually edged by a fine red line.

Range in PNW: Western and central Oregon southward into California

Habitat: Brushlands

Host plants: Species of currant (*Ribes*)

The Tailed Copper is distinctive in appearance and uncommon. The tails may lead you to think of a hairstreak, but the upper surfaces, slightly iridescent in the male and splotchy and two-toned in the female, are typical of a copper. The crisp pattern of the underside distinguishes this species definitively from any other copper. I've seen the Tailed Copper at Bly Mountain Pass, Klamath County on July 2 (it snowed the next day), and in the Warner Mountains just east of Lakeview, where this photograph was taken. Don't expect to see a lot of them anywhere.

DOUG HEPBURN

Blue Copper   *Lycaena heteronea*

Wingspan: 1⅛–1¼ inches

Description: In males, the **top** is iridescent violet-blue; in females, the top is a cool slate brown with black spots. The **underside** is ivory with black spots on the forewing and sometimes on the hindwing.

Range in PNW: Cascade Mountains eastward

Habitat: Mountain meadows and mountaintops

Host plants: Species of buckwheat (*Eriogonum*)

Here is a copper that is not copper-colored. In fact, the male is blue enough to make you think it's a blue. The female looks something like the female Ruddy Copper but has a cooler hue. The Blue Copper is an avid visitor of flowers in mountain meadows. The one shown here with its wings held together vertically is feeding on buckwheat, which is also the host plant of the Blue Copper's caterpillar. Not all individuals have spots on the hindwing. The male on the aster displays the handsome lilac sheen of the upper surface.

DOUG HEPBURN

DOUG HEPBURN

Purplish Copper   *Lycaena helloides*

Wingspan: 1–1 ⅛ inches

Description: In males, the **top** is iridescent purplish brown with submarginal orange crescents on the hindwing; in females, the top is dull orange, spotted and streaked with black. The **underside** of the hindwing is violet-brown with a submarginal wavy orange line.

Range in PNW: Throughout

Habitat: Meadows and marshy areas

Host plants: Species of dock (*Rumex*) and knotweed (*Polygonum*)

The Pacific Northwest's most widespread copper, this is the only one that frequents moist valleys west of the Cascades. The Purplish Copper looks something like the Lilac-bordered Copper but has a darker underside marked by a prominent squiggly orange line, well illustrated in the photograph on the right. The marshy setting of that photo is typical habitat for this species. The other picture shows a male from the top.

DOUG HEPBURN

DOUG HEPBURN

Lilac-bordered Copper   *Lycaena nivalis*

Wingspan: 1–1⅛ inches

Description: In males, the **top** is iridescent purplish brown with submarginal orange crescents on the hindwing; in females, the top is dull orange and has black spots and streaks. The **underside** of the hindwing has a yellow inner half and a violet outer half. In some populations the underside is bright and colorful; in others, pale and indistinctly marked.

Range in PNW: Cascade Mountains eastward and Olympic Mountains

Habitat: Mountain meadows and prairies

Host plants: Knotweed (*Polygonum douglasii*)

The Lilac-bordered Copper is a common mountain butterfly. It's found in flowery meadows near the forest or on rocky ridges above timberline. I've seen plenty of them from mid-June through August on the Grasshopper Pass Trail in the North Cascades, in Tronsen Meadows in the Wenatchee Mountains, on the ridge of Steens Mountain hanging over Kiger Gorge, on flowers along roads through the Ochoco Mountains, and all over the broad subalpine reaches of Mount Ashland. The butterfly on the right is a female.

DOUG HEPBURN

WILLIAM NEILL

Mariposa Copper   *Lycaena mariposa*

Wingspan: 1−1⅛ inches

Description: In males, the **top** is iridescent purplish brown; in females, the top is dull orange with black spots and a black submarginal area. The **underside** of the hindwing is streaked gray with transverse rows of wavy black lines.

Range in PNW: Cascade Mountains eastward and Olympic Mountains

Habitat: Mountain forests

Host plants: Species of blueberry (*Vaccinium*)

The streaked gray hindwing of the Mariposa Copper is well illustrated in this photograph. No other small butterfly in our region has this feature. Mariposas fly where blueberries thrive in open high mountain forests. Some individuals are still on the wing, flitting among the late wildflowers, when the first snow falls on the high trails of the Cascade Crest. Textured, turban-shaped eggs are fastened to blueberry stems, where they remain through the winter. The green, sluglike caterpillars hatch in the spring.

HAIRSTREAKS and ELFINS _____

Coral Hairstreak   *Satyrium titus*
A.k.a., *Harkenclenus titus*

Wingspan: ⅞–1¼ inches

Description: The **top** is grayish brown. The **underside** of the hindwing is light grayish brown with a submarginal row of red-orange spots. In males, the forewing is triangular with a pointed apex; females are larger and have a more rounded outline.

Range in PNW: East of Cascade Mountains

Habitat: Brushlands and disturbed woods

Host plants: Cherry and plum trees (both *Prunus*)

The Coral Hairstreak's row of conspicuous orange spots is distinctive. This species occurs across the United States, but in our area it is not common and does not reach west of the Cascades. Poke around among the scruffy patches of chokecherry where U.S. 97 crosses some creeks south of Toppenish, along the Okanogan River almost to the Canadian border, or on the way to Cornucopia on the south side of the Wallowa Mountains. Check the chokecherry flowers for butterflies. Eggs overwinter, green caterpillars hatch in the spring, and adults fly in early summer.

WILLIAM NEILL

California Hairstreak   *Satyrium californicum*

A.k.a., *S. californica*

Wingspan: 1–1⅛ inches

Description: The **top** is brown with orange spots near the base of the hind-wing tail; in females, the spots extend along the submarginal area, often onto the forewing. The **underside** is pale brown with black spots. On the hindwing, a blue spot at the base of the tail is flanked by orange crescents that diminish as they extend along the submarginal area.

Range in PNW: Cascade Mountains eastward and Siskiyou Mountains southward

Habitat: Brushlands and low mountains

Host plants: Bitterbrush (*Purshia tridentata*)

The underside of a female is shown here, with the submarginal orange spots reaching from the hindwing tail all along the forewing. The orange and blue near the hindwing tail are field marks that help identify this butterfly as a California Hairstreak, but from her standpoint, the marks serve as protective coloration. The tail and its associated bright spots are meant to look like a head, enticing predators to strike at this nonvital part of the butterfly.

DOUG HEPBURN

WILLIAM NEILL

Sylvan Hairstreak   *Satyrium sylvinum*

A.k.a., *S. sylvinus*

> **Wingspan:** 1–1⅛ inches
>
> **Description:** The **top** is brown with orange spots at the base of the hindwing tail. The **underside** is pale gray-brown with black spots. On the hindwing a blue spot is flanked by small red-orange crescents that sometimes extend as faint orange marks along the rest of the submarginal area of the hindwing.
>
> **Range in PNW:** Cascade Mountains eastward and Siskiyou Mountains southward
>
> **Habitat:** Streamsides and brushlands
>
> **Host plants:** Species of willow (*Salix*)

Compare this photograph to the one of the California Hairstreak. Both are females. The underside of the Sylvan Hairstreak has smaller black spots, red-orange marks that do not extend as far from the hindwing tail, and, in many individuals, a gray, not brownish, background color. Both species inhabit dry scrubby land, fly during July, and visit flowers avidly. The Sylvan Hairstreak uses willow as a host plant, so it is perhaps more often seen near streams, but the two species often occur together there as well.

WILLIAM NEILL

Hedgerow Hairstreak   *Satyrium saepium*

Wingspan: 1–1 ⅛ inches

Description: The **top** is deep red-brown. The **underside** is pale gray-brown with an irregular transverse white-edged black line. A faint blue spot at the base of the hindwing tail is flanked by two black spots.

Range in PNW: Cascade Mountains eastward and Siskiyou Mountains southward

Habitat: Open forest brushlands

Host plants: Species of *Ceanothus*

The entire upper surface of the wings, in males and females alike, is saturated with an intense bright rust color, which sets this butterfly apart from other hairstreaks. The underside—the side we usually see first—is comparatively tame, so the flash of hot color when the butterfly takes off is always startling. This is a common butterfly on the eastern slope of the Cascades and in the Siskiyous, especially if you're within sight of ceanothus bushes. There is a long flight period from late June until the end of August. The pale green caterpillar blends in with the underside of a ceanothus leaf.

DOUG HEPBURN

WILLIAM NEILL

Mountain Mahogany Hairstreak *Satyrium tetra*
A.k.a., *S. adenostomatis*

Wingspan: 1–1⅛ inches

Description: The wings are triangular with blunt hindwing tails. The **top** is dark brownish gray. The **underside** is gray-brown dusted by white scales that obscure the following subtle hindwing markings: a faint broken transverse white line, submarginal small black triangles, and a barely discernible blue spot at the anal angle.

Range in PNW: South-central Oregon southward into California

Habitat: Brushlands on mountain hillsides

Host plants: Species of mountain mahogany (*Cercocarpus*)

The host plants of the Mountain Mahogany Hairstreak grow on arid foothills of mountains in California and southern Oregon. This somber little butterfly can be seen in July sipping nectar on the rabbitbrush that grows so profusely along Oregon 31 where the two-lane blacktop runs between the western shore of Summer Lake and the steep slopes of Winter Ridge. The underside of this hairstreak looks something like that of the Hedgerow Hairstreak, but flecks of white scales are visible on fresh individuals, and colors of the upper sides are completely different. Overwintering takes place in the egg stage.

WILLIAM NEILL

Sooty Hairstreak   *Satyrium fuliginosum*

Wingspan: ⅞–1⅛ inches

Description: The **top** is gray-brown, and the **underside** is a gray-brown tweed with rows of black spots rimmed in white.

Range in PNW: Cascade Mountains southward into California and eastward into mountains of Idaho

Habitat: Mountain meadows and alpine areas

Host plants: Species of lupine (*Lupinus*)

The name Sooty Hairstreak aptly describes this drab butterfly. The gray and brown scales are mixed in a way that gives the wings a dirty look in worn individuals and a tweedy look in fresh ones. The only markings are indistinct spots on the underside, which can be mistaken for those of a tattered Boisduval's Blue. Take a hike above timberline at Cloud Cap on Mount Hood to enjoy the view in midsummer and you'll be walking past Sooty Hairstreaks on the ground-level buckwheat blossoms you're taking care not to tread on.

DOUG HEPBURN

Behr's Hairstreak   *Satyrium behrii*

Wingspan: ⅞–1 inch

Description: The **top** is pale orange with wide brown borders. The **underside** is gray-brown with white-edged angular marks forming strong lines and triangles.

Range in PNW: Cascade Mountains eastward and southward into Nevada

Habitat: Arid mountain foothills

Host plants: Bitterbrush (*Purshia tridentata*)

You'll recognize Behr's Hairstreak by its two-toned top and the distinctive white-edged black marks on the underside. The butterfly pictured here is resting on bitterbrush growing in the hot, dusty terrain this hairstreak likes— slopes where pine forest gives way to scattered juniper and then to prairie. You'll find these butterflies along forest roads near Indian Ford Campground in central Oregon and along the highway between Bend and Klamath Falls.

Gray Hairstreak   *Strymon melinus*

Wingspan: ⅞–1⅛ inches

Description: The **top** is dark gray with a large orange crescent at the base of the long hindwing tail. The **underside** is pale gray with a transverse white-edged black line and one or two orange crescents at the base of the hindwing tail.

Range in PNW: Throughout

Habitat: Many

Host plants: Legumes, species of mallow (*Malva*), and others

The orange spots adjacent to the hindwing tail are somewhat like those of other hairstreaks, but the Gray Hairstreak's orange spots are brighter, and the pallor of the gray underside is distinctive. The elaborate hindwing pattern serves as a decoy. Black and white lines guide the predator's attention to the conspicuous false eyespot. The long delicate tails move with the breeze and simulate antennae. The green caterpillar pictured here is dining on mallow.

WILLIAM NEILL

WILLIAM NEILL

Bramble Green Hairstreak   *Callophrys perplexa*

A.k.a., Bramble Hairstreak, *C. dumetorum*

Wingspan: ⅞–1 inch

Description: The **top** is gray-brown in males and warm brown in females. The hindwing has a blunt tail. The **underside** is bright apple green with a transverse row of faint white marks.

Range in PNW: Cascade Mountains from southern Washington to central Oregon then westward, and Siskiyou Mountains southward into California

Habitat: Open forests and brushlands

Host plants: Species of *Lotus*, including deer vetch (*L. nevadensis*)

Hairstreaks with green undersides occur in many colonies in varied habitats across the Pacific Northwest. Their bright green color makes them, as a group, easy to recognize in the field, but separating them into species is difficult, and their nomenclature is in flux. This book presents two relatively well-defined species, the Bramble Green Hairstreak and the Sheridan's Green Hairstreak. They differ slightly in appearance and flight period, and their host plants are unrelated (which may explain why the species usually do not occur in the same place). The Bramble Green Hairstreak frequents open pine forests along the eastern foothills of the Cascades in northern Oregon and southern Washington. It is closely associated with deer vetch, a prostrate lotus plant with small round leaves and yellow flowers, upon which I have found its eggs. In these areas, adults fly around Memorial Day.

DOUG HEPBURN

WILLIAM NEILL

Sheridan's Green Hairstreak   *Callophrys sheridanii*

A.k.a., Sheridan's Hairstreak

Wingspan: ⅞–1 inch

Description: The **top** is gray-brown in both genders. The hindwing has a blunt tail. The **underside** is bright bluish green with a transverse row of white marks, occasionally merged into a continuous line.

Range in PNW: East of Cascade Mountains

Habitat: Canyons and rocky hillsides

Host plants: Species of buckwheat (*Eriogonum*), including *E. compositum*

Compared with the Bramble Green Hairstreak's yellowish green tone, Sheridan's Green Hairstreak typically has a bluish green hue. Also, females are not warm brown on top, but that's not likely to help you with identification in the field since they never alight with their top surface displayed. Sheridan's Green Hairstreak is found east of the Cascades in rocky canyons where buckwheat grows. It flies early in the season, March and April. Look for its caterpillars in May. They are bright green like the buckwheat leaves they eat, but they give themselves away by scraping off only the top surface of the tough leaf, leaving a telltale bright green blemish.

DOUG HEPBURN

WILLIAM NEILL

Cedar Hairstreak *Mitoura grynea*

A.k.a., Juniper Hairstreak, Nelson's Hairstreak, *Callophys grynea*

Wingspan: ⅞–1 inch

Description: The **top** is brown, and the hindwing has a white-tipped tail. On the **underside** of the hindwing, an incomplete transverse white line separates the bluish submarginal area from the larger brown-violet basal area.

Range in PNW: Throughout

Habitat: Conifer forests

Host plants: Western red cedar (*Thuja plicata*), species of juniper (*Juniperus*)

The key field mark of the Cedar Hairstreak is the beautiful violet hues on the underside, which are variable depending on the locale and best seen on a fresh individual in bright sunlight. Compared to Johnson's Hairstreak, the transverse white line on the Cedar Hairstreak's hindwing is not so bold. Adults are fond of strawberry blossoms, desert parsley, buckwheat, and groundsel. Females emerge from hibernated pupae in May and later fasten their eggs to the scalelike needles of their food plant. The mature green and white caterpillar is handsome, as shown.

Thicket Hairstreak   *Mitoura spinetorum*

A.k.a., *Callophrys spinetorum*

Wingspan: 1–1⅛ inches

Description: The **top** is dark blue and slightly iridescent. The hindwing has a white-tipped tail. The **underside** of the hindwing is reddish chocolate brown with a jagged zigzag transverse white line. There are faint orange crescents and blue scaling in the submarginal area.

Range in PNW: Cascade Mountains eastward

Habitat: Conifer forests

Host plants: Species of conifer mistletoe (*Arceuthobium*), usually on pine trees

The satiny steel blue upper surface of the Thicket Hairstreak is unlike that of any other butterfly in our area. Distinguishing this species from Johnson's Hairstreak on the basis of the underside alone can't reliably be done. However, the zigs on the zigzag white line are more pointed in the Thicket Hairstreak. Also, the row of black spots just distal to this line is usually comprised of just three spots in Johnson's Hairstreak but extends almost all the way around the wing's outer margin in the Thicket. The Thicket Hairstreak, a forest butterfly, occurs sparingly in scattered colonies. Occasionally you'll see them on ceanothus or other flowers or sunning on a dirt road through the forest, but adults spend most of their time high in the trees. Pupae, only tenuously entangled with mistletoe and lichen, sometimes fall to the ground.

DOUG HEPBURN

WILLIAM NEILL

DOUG HEPBURN

Johnson's Hairstreak   *Mitoura johnsoni*

Wingspan: 1⅛–1¼ inches

Description: The **top** is chocolate brown. The hindwing has a white-tipped tail. The hindwing **underside** is reddish brown with a zigzag transverse white line and blue and red marks near the base of the tail.

Range in PNW: Coast Range and Cascade Mountains southward into California, and Wallowa Mountains

Habitat: Conifer forests

Host plants: Mistletoe (*Arceuthobium campylopodum*), usually on hemlock

Like the Thicket Hairstreak, Johnson's Hairstreak inhabits conifer forests infested with its host plant, mistletoe. While the Thicket uses mistletoe that grows on pine, Johnson's Hairstreak prefers mistletoe growing on hemlock. Adults of both species live mainly high in the trees, seldom descending to where we would see them. You may have more luck seeing eggs or caterpillars. Look for them on young hemlock trees with mistletoe that's low enough to reach. Eggs are fastened to the mistletoe or to adjacent conifer branches. Look sharply; the mottled green and brown caterpillars are marvelously camouflaged.

DOUG HEPBURN

WILLIAM NEILL

WILLIAM NEILL

Western Pine Elfin   *Incisalia eryphon*

A.k.a., *Callophrys eryphon*

Wingspan: ⅞–1⅛ inches

Description: The **top** is gray-brown in males and warm brown in females. The hindwing has a blunt tail and scalloped edges. The **underside** of the hindwing is brown tinged with purple and has rows of angular dark lines, which form sharp points. The wing fringes are checkered in black and white.

Range in PNW: Throughout

Habitat: Conifer forests

Host plants: Pine trees (*Pinus*), including ponderosa and lodgepole

The Western Pine Elfin is brown with a striking pattern of repeating triangles on the underside. The male in the photo, demonstrating typical behavior, is perched on a pine bough on the lookout for a passing female. As you make your way through the woods, watch for these butterflies on the branches of young pines to the side of the path. They dart from their perch to inspect you. Pine Elfin caterpillars burrow into new growth at the end of pine twigs.

DOUG HEPBURN

Brown Elfin   *Incisalia augustinus*

A.k.a., *Callophrys augustinus*

Wingspan: ⅞–1 inch

Description: The **top** is brown. The hindwing has a blunt tail. The **underside** of the hindwing has an irregular white line separating the dark brown inner region from the pale pinkish brown outer region.

Range in PNW: Throughout

Habitat: Forests and brushlands

Host plants: Salal (*Gaultheria shallon*), bitterbrush (*Purshia tridentata*), manzanita (*Arctostaphylos*), species of blueberry (*Vaccinium*), and others

The wings of the Brown Elfin are colored with a limited palette: variations of brown. In the photograph, last year's flower head seems precarious for this butterfly, but it provides a panoramic view and a launching pad unobstructed in any direction. Look for this species in the spring on flowers and moist ground along roads through the forest. At that time, the adults visit the flowers of blueberry, kinnikinnick, and other host plants of its caterpillar.

WILLIAM NEILL

Moss's Elfin   *Incisalia mossii*

A.k.a., *Callophrys mossii*

Wingspan: ⅞–1 inch

Description: The **top** is brown. The hindwing has a blunt tail. The **underside** of the hindwing has an irregular transverse white line separating the inner dark brown region from the lighter outer region; this outer region contains pinkish or bluish scales. The wing fringe are white.

Range in PNW: Throughout

Habitat: Rock outcroppings

Host plants: Species of stonecrop, including *Sedum spathulifolium*

Although its pattern resembles that of the Brown Elfin, Moss's Elfin has a distinct transverse white line on the hindwing, and its wings are fringed with white. Look for this butterfly near rock outcroppings and other exposed sunny places where sedum grows. Adults emerge early in the spring—at low altitudes in early March, and in the mountains while patches of snow still linger nearby. Moss's Elfins usually rest on the ground, not showing much interest in flowers. Eggs are most often attached to a sedum stem that is bearing flower buds, and the newly hatched caterpillars crawl up to hide within the flower head. The caterpillar in the picture is fully grown.

WILLIAM NEILL

WILLIAM NEILL

Hoary Elfin   *Incisalia polios*
A.k.a., *Callophrys polios*

Wingspan: ⅞–1 inch

Description: The **top** is brown. The hindwing has a blunt tail. On the **underside** of the hindwing a basal brown region is separated from a lighter outer region by a distinct irregular border. The outer region is suffused with white scales, especially toward the edge of the wing.

Range in PNW: Scattered local colonies in Washington and Oregon, extending into Idaho and Canada

Habitat: Open conifer forests and brushlands

Host plants: Kinnikinnick (*Arctostaphylos uva-ursi*)

The heavy suffusion of white scales gives the underside of the Hoary Elfin's hindwing a bluish cast, which is the basis for the butterfly's common name. You can find this elfin in April on kinnikinnick-covered mounds near Tenino, Washington, and later in May in the pine forest between Lehman Springs and Bally Mountain in northeastern Oregon. Patches of kinnickinnick are always nearby whenever the butterfly is sighted.

DOUG HEPBURN

Golden Hairstreak *Habrodais grunus*

A.k.a., Chinquapin Hairstreak

Wingspan: 1⅛–1⅜ inches

Description: The **top** is golden yellow with brown outer borders, which are wider in males. The hindwing has a short tail. The **underside** is pale yellow with faint linear reddish brown marks.

Range in PNW: Cascade Mountains from Columbia Gorge southward into California

Habitat: Forests

Host plants: Chinquapin (*Castanopsis chrysophylla*), species of oak (*Quercus*)

The Golden Hairstreak is the only plain golden yellow butterfly in the Pacific Northwest. In Oregon, the host plant is chinquapin. In California, oaks are used. Pale blue eggs are attached to the undersides of leaves, often near the top of the tallest branch on the bush. Eggs overwinter and do not hatch until tender new leaves emerge on the hairstreak's evergreen host plant late in the spring. Adults fly in August and September, using chinquapin as a nectar source, as seen in the photograph.

DOUG HEPBURN

DOUG HEPBURN

WILLIAM NEILL

BLUES

Silvery Blue *Glaucopsyche lygdamus*

Wingspan: ⅞–1⅛ inches

Description: In males, the **top** is bright silvery blue; in females, the blue color is suffused with black. The **underside** is pale gray spattered with round black spots of uniform size circled by narrow white rings.

Range in PNW: Throughout

Habitat: Meadows

Host plants: Species of lupine (*Lupinus*)

For a bright shiny blue color, the male Silvery Blue (left) outdoes all other blues. The iridescence results from the prismatic structure of the wing scales. The mating pair in the photo (the browner female is on the left) demonstrates the distinctive field mark of this species on the underside of the wings, the round black spots circled in white. This common meadow butterfly is at home in the mountains as well as in farmland. Adult Silvery Blues—at least those at low altitude—fly early in the spring. Apparently the species hibernates as a pupa (unusual for a blue), which may help the adult get an early start.

DOUG HEPBURN

DOUG HEPBURN

Arrowhead Blue *Glaucopsyche piasus*

Wingspan: 1–1⅛ inches

Description: The **top** is dark purplish blue with checkered wing fringes. The **underside** is gray with large black spots; the hindwing has white arrowheads pointed toward the body.

Range in PNW: Cascade Mountains eastward

Habitat: Prairies and open forests

Host plants: Species of lupine (*Lupinus*)

The Arrowhead Blue has a unique underside, making it easy to identify. It's also large for a blue. In most species of blues, the gender can be determined at a glance: males are bright blue on top; females, darker blue or brown. With this species, however, it's hard to tell a male from a female. Arrowhead Blues are attracted to mud and visit flowers for nectar, but you seldom see more than one at a time.

DOUG HEPBURN

Greenish Blue *Plebejus saepiolus*

Wingspan: ⅞–1⅛ inches

Description: The **top** is greenish blue in males and brown in females. The **underside** is bluish gray in males and tan in females. The underside has numerous black spots and sometimes minute submarginal red crescents, seen more often in females.

Range in PNW: Throughout, but sparse west of Cascade Crest

Habitat: Wet meadows

Host plants: Species of clover (*Trifolium*)

The upper side of the male Greenish Blue (right) is imbued with a blue sheen that ranges from sparkling cerulean to lilac depending on the angle of sunlight reflected from the prismatic wing scales. The colors of the forewing and hindwing appear to differ in our picture because the butterfly is holding the wings at different angles. The photo on the left shows a female on a clover blossom, the Greenish Blue's host plant. Her proboscis is not uncoiled for feeding. Instead, her abdomen is thrust forward, perhaps about to deposit an egg on the flower petal. Females stick their disk-shaped blue eggs onto clover flower heads.

DOUG HEPBURN

WILLIAM NEILL

Boisduval's Blue   *Icaricia icarioides*

A.k.a., Common Blue, *Plebejus icarioides*

Wingspan: 1–1 ⅛ inches

Description: In males, the **top** is blue; in females, the blue color is suffused with black. The gray **underside** is spotted. On the forewing, the spots are black with narrow white rims; on the hindwing, the spots are mainly white with smaller black centers.

Range in PNW: Throughout

Habitat: Mountain meadows and prairies

Host plants: Species of lupine (*Lupinus*)

To distinguish Boisduval's Blue from the Silvery Blue, look to the white-rimmed black spots on the underside. In Boisduval's Blue, the spots are mainly black on the forewing and mainly white on the hindwing. In the Silvery Blue, the spots are the same on both wings. Boisduval's Blue is widespread and numerous, sometimes crowding together in groups to drink from wet ground along footpaths through the forest. Females lay eggs in early summer. The caterpillars forage briefly, then enter diapause until the following spring, when they complete their development. The photos show a violet-brown caterpillar before diapause and a mature green caterpillar early in the spring.

A subspecies or variety of this butterfly named Fender's Blue (top right) once inhabited the Willamette Valley grasslands, using a local native plant, Kincaid's lupine, as its host. As the valley was farmed and urbanized, the grasslands were all but eliminated. Now, Fender's Blue is relegated to meager remnants of its original habitat where Kincaid's lupine hangs on. Both plant and butterfly are federally listed as endangered species. In Fender's Blue, the black spots on the underside are small and the white rims around them are much abbreviated, making its appearance more like that of the Silvery Blue.

DOUG HEPBURN

DOUG HEPBURN

WILLIAM NEILL

WILLIAM NEILL

Acmon Blue   *Icaricia acmon*

A.k.a., *Plebejus acmon*

> **Wingspan:** ¾–1 inch
>
> **Description:** The **top**, which is blue in males and brown in females, has a submarginal orange band on the hindwing. The **underside** is gray with black spots. The underside of the hindwing has a row of submarginal orange crescents (or a confluent orange band) capped at the periphery by blue-green iridescent spots.
>
> **Range in PNW:** Throughout, except in western Washington lowlands
>
> **Habitat:** Prairies
>
> **Host plants:** Species of buckwheat (*Eriogonum*)

The Acmon Blue is distinguished by its pattern of blue and orange on the top and underside of the wings, which is present in both genders. The photographs demonstrate this well, although the iridescent spots on the underside are more striking when the sun hits them at just the right angle. This butterfly is common, especially on dry foothills that come down to the prairie. There are two broods, so you'll spot adults at flowers and mud anytime from May through September.

WILLIAM NEILL

DOUG HEPBURN

Shasta Blue   *Icaricia shasta*

A.k.a., *Plebejus shasta*

Wingspan: ⅞–1 inch

Description: In males, the **top** is purplish blue; in females, the blue is suffused with brown. The **underside** is gray with white wing veins, and the hindwing has a submarginal row of iridescent blue-green spots capped centrally by white triangles and a speck of orange.

Range in PNW: Cascade Mountains in central Oregon southward into California and eastward to Steens Mountain

Habitat: Forest openings and alpine regions

Host plants: Species of lupine (*Lupinus*), *Astragalus,* and *Lotus*

You can identify the Shasta Blue by its underside: white wing veins and metallic spots abutted by white triangles. We took this photo at 9,000 feet on Steens Mountain, where the colony seems to be concentrated within a few hundred feet of the ridge overlooking the desert a vertical mile below. To avoid the unremitting wind, these tiny blues were restricting their flight to only a few inches above the ground. This little butterfly is at home amid the rigorous conditions of mountain peaks and takes its name from Mount Shasta. Yet isolated colonies also occur in central Oregon on level meadows surrounded by forest at about 5,000 feet elevation.

DOUG HEPBURN

Melissa Blue   *Lycaeides melissa*

A.k.a., *Plebejus melissa*

Wingspan: ⅞–1 inch

Description: In males, the **top** is intense lavender blue without markings; in females, the top is brown with a submarginal orange band on all the wings. The **underside** is gray with black spots and a submarginal orange band (or crescents) capped on the hindwing by blue-green iridescent spots.

Range in PNW: East of Cascade Mountains

Habitat: Arid prairies and mountain meadows

Host plants: Species of lupine (*Lupinus*), *Astragalus*, and *Lotus*

The orange and blue-green markings of the Melissa Blue are like those of the Acmon Blue, but their distribution differs. On its underside, the Melissa Blue has orange on all wings of both genders, but the orange is repeated on the top of females only. Males are plain blue on top. The photographs show the top of a female (left) and the underside of a male (right). A Melissa Blue caterpillar, tended by ants, is pictured on page 19.

DOUG HEPBURN

WILLIAM NEILL

Northern Blue   *Lycaeides idas*

A.k.a., Idas Blue, *Plebejus idas*

Wingspan: ⅞–1⅛ inches

Description: In males, the **top** is intense lavender blue without markings; in females, the top is brown with faint submarginal orange crescents on all the wings. The **underside** is pale powdery gray with faint submarginal orange and iridescent blue-green marks.

Range in PNW: Cascade, Olympic, and Wallowa Mountains

Habitat: High mountain meadows

Host plants: Species of lupine (*Lupinus*)

The Northern Blue's design is essentially the same as that of the Melissa Blue, but all markings are much fainter—so much so that, at first glance, the underside looks white, not spotted. In the photograph, one of the butterflies, a male, has parted his wings enough to reveal a glimpse of the blue upper surface. The Northern Blue is common in montane meadows of the Cascade Mountains, while the Melissa Blue prefers the mountains to the east and is not as partial to high altitude.

DOUG HEPBURN

Square-spotted Blue   *Euphilotes battoides*
A.k.a., Battoides Blue, Bat Blue

Wingspan: ¾–1 inch

Description: In males, the **top** is purplish blue with black borders, sometimes with faint submarginal orange spots on the hindwing; in females, the top is brown with a submarginal orange band on the hindwing. The **underside** is gray with black spots, which are large and square on the forewing; there is a submarginal orange band on the hindwing.

Range in PNW: Cascade and Siskiyou Mountains eastward and southward

Habitat: Arid prairies and arid mountains

Host plants: Species of buckwheat (*Eriogonum*)

The Square-spotted Blue has orange on the underside of the hindwing like the Acmon Blue, but no adjacent iridescent spots. The butterfly taking nectar from a yellow buckwheat blossom, photographed at 5,000 feet in the high desert, has the exceptionally large black spots characteristic of this species. The other photo shows a Square-spotted Blue sitting on alpine vegetation at the 9,000-foot summit of Steens Mountain. I've seen these little blues taking nourishment from coyote or dog scat on dusty trails high in the Cascade Mountains.

DOUG HEPBURN

DOUG HEPBURN

Arctic Blue   *Agriades glandon*

Wingspan: 7/8–1 inch

Description: In males, the **top** has a semitransparent thin layer of silvery blue scales and a submarginal row of black spots on the hindwing; in females, the top is grayish brown and also thinly clad, allowing markings to show through from the underside. The **underside** has black spots enclosed by white rims and white confluent patches, plus a speck of submarginal orange.

Range in PNW: Cascade and Olympic Mountains northward into Canada

Habitat: Moist mountain meadows

Host plants: Species of shooting star (*Dodecatheon*) and saxifrage (*Saxifraga*), including spotted saxifrage (*S. bronchialis*)

The Arctic Blue is an alpine butterfly that occurs in isolated colonies near or above timberline. The photo at top right illustrates how the underside markings show through the wings. The mature caterpillar shown is eating the leaves of spotted saxifrage. One day in early August, exploring an alpine ridge in the North Cascades, I found several white eggs attached to the basal leaves of a saxifrage plant that was part of a mat growing between rocks. Curious about the species, I took some of the eggs home and raised them. The caterpillars that hatched ate saxifrage leaves for a short while, then became inactive and refused food, preparing to hibernate. After a winter in the refrigerator, they resumed eating the next spring and matured into Arctic Blues.

DOUG HEPBURN

DOUG HEPBURN

WILLIAM NEILL

Spring Azure *Celastrina argiolus*
A.k.a., Echo Blue, *C. echo, C. ladon*

Wingspan: ⅞–1 inch

Description: In males, the **top** is blue; in females, the blue is suffused with black, especially on the forewing apex. The **underside** is pale gray with white streaks, small black spots, and a submarginal fine, wavy black line.

Range in PNW: Throughout

Habitat: Open forests and other varied habitats

Host plants: Buds, flowers, and fruits of woody bushes, including ocean spray (*Holodiscus discolor*) and species of dogwood (*Cornus*), elderberry (*Sambucus*), and cherry (*Prunus*)

The delicate markings and absence of any orange characterize the Spring Azure. Caterpillars eat the buds and blossoms of a wide variety of flowering shrubs, which may explain its ability to coexist with humans in our city landscaping. On Memorial Day, I watched several females flitting over osier dogwood bushes growing along a riverbank. They would pause at a flower head, stepping carefully among the buds, then more often than not depart as if unsatisfied. At length, when one of them found the right conditions, she deftly wedged her abdomen between the buds and pasted an egg on the side of one, where it was well hidden. The caterpillars that hatched ate the buds and flowers and were willing to switch to the flowers of several other shrubs, but they turned down any foliage I offered, including dogwood.

DOUG HEPBURN

WILLIAM NEILL

Western Tailed Blue   *Everes amyntula*

Wingspan: ⅞–1 inch

Description: In males, the **top** is purplish blue; in females, the blue is suffused with black. The **underside** is pale bluish gray with little black spots. The underside of the hindwing has a minute orange and iridescent blue spot at the base of its delicate tail.

Range in PNW: Throughout

Habitat: Forest meadows and streamsides

Host plants: Legumes, including species of *Astragalus, Lotus,* and *Lathyrus*

Only one blue has tails: the Western Tailed Blue. Newly hatched individuals are powdery white on the underside. In an older, smudged individual whose tails have broken off—which occurs often—the minute orange and iridescent spot on the hindwing may help distinguish it from the Silvery Blue and Spring Azure. Its favored habitats are meadows and openings in moist forest, often near watercourses. The Western Tailed Blue is also at home in disturbed territory around farms and towns. In spring I have watched females fasten their disk-shaped white eggs on stems at the base of vetch blossoms. Newborn caterpillars move into the flowers to hide.

DOUG HEPBURN

METALMARKS

Mormon Metalmark *Apodemia mormo*

Wingspan: 1–1¼ inches

Description: The antennae are long and the wing fringes are checkered. The **top** is black spotted with white and has a copper patch on the forewing. The **underside** is streaked light gray and brown with white spots and has an orange forewing patch.

Range in PNW: East of Cascade Mountains southward into California

Habitat: Arid prairies and canyons

Host plants: Species of buckwheat (*Eriogonum*), including *E. compositum* and *E. strictum*

The Mormon Metalmark is the Pacific Northwest's only representative of this family of mainly tropical butterflies. Adults fly in September, when their arid surroundings lie scorched by the summer. The buckwheat species *Eriogonum strictum* blooms at that time in the canyons and serves as a nectar source as well as a larval host plant. Conical lavender eggs deposited on the stems and leaves of buckwheat lie dormant during the winter. Caterpillars hatch in April to eat new foliage. Mature caterpillars are purple and covered by fine hairs.

DOUG HEPBURN

DOUG HEPBURN

WILLIAM NEILL

FRITILLARIES

Sorting out the fritillaries is apt to be a humbling experience. When I call out the species name of a fritillary I'm watching, I attach the word *probably*. They are wonderful butterflies, but there is so little difference between the species and so much variability within them that I'm often unsure of what I'm looking at. Should you fret over this fickleness of biology or exalt in the generosity of nature's beauty? I advise against fretting. It's an achievement to simply recognize a butterfly as a fritillary, at least in the beginning.

Callippe Fritillary   *Speyeria callippe*

Wingspan: 2–2⅜ inches

Description: The **top** is yellowish orange-brown with black marks, usually heavy. Pale ovals on top overlie the silver spots on the other side of the wings. The **underside** of the hindwing is brownish and usually smeared with green (but not in the Siskiyou Mountains or on Mount Adams); the silver spots are large and elongated into ovals.

Range in PNW: Cascade and Siskiyou Mountains eastward

Habitat: Prairies, mountains, and alpine areas

Host plants: Species of violet (*Viola*), including *V. nuttallii*

Most Callippe Fritillaries have some green on the underside, and their bold silver spots are more elongated than in other species. Pale ovals on the top of the wings overlie the silver spots on the other side to some extent in all fritillaries, but more so in Callippes, especially females. Callippe habitat reaches into alpine areas. Males hoping to rendezvous with mates congregate in summer at the 9,000-foot summit of Strawberry Mountain and on the dizzying ridges of Aneroid Mountain in the Wallowa Mountains.

DOUG HEPBURN

DOUG HEPBURN

Hydaspe Fritillary   *Speyeria hydaspe*

Wingspan: 2–2¼ inches

Description: The **top** is orange-brown or tawny, with heavy black marks. The **underside** of the hindwing is purplish brown or maroon with a paler submarginal band; the spots are ochre, sometimes lightly silvered.

Range in PNW: Throughout, except Columbia Basin in Washington and desert in southeastern Oregon

Habitat: Forests

Host plants: Species of violet (*Viola*), including *V. adunca* and *V. nuttallii*

Hydaspe is the easiest fritillary to identify: the underside of its hindwing is maroon or purplish and has spots that usually are not silvered. The most common fritillary in mountain forests, it is often found along the roads that run through the Coast Range. The seasonal timing of the life cycle is the same for all of the large fritillaries (genus *Speyeria*). Fertilized females fasten their eggs to some firm surface adjacent to the withered remains of violet plants during August and September. Caterpillars hatch from the eggs in a week or two and eat their eggshells but nothing else during the first summer. These tiny animals, looking like a bit of black thread, disappear into the leaf litter to spend the end of summer, fall, and winter in diapause, living entirely off metabolic resources their mother provided in the egg. The caterpillars become active in the spring and begin eating violet leaves for the first time. Although there must be a lot of caterpillars, they are difficult to find; some believe they eat mainly at night and hide during the day. The photo shows a mature caterpillar. Pupation is carried out near the ground. The photograph of the pupa was taken after cutting away a portion of the pupa's shelter, which consisted of dead leaves tied together with silk.

WILLIAM NEILL

DOUG HEPBURN

DOUG HEPBURN

WILLIAM NEILL

Zerene Fritillary *Speyeria zerene*

Wingspan: 2⅛–2⅜ inches

Description: The **top** is orange-brown with heavy black marks. The color on the **underside** of the hindwing is variable, ranging from ochre at Steens Mountain to brown with an ochre submarginal band in the Siskiyou Mountains and at Mount Adams. They have large silver spots on the underside of the hindwing, except in southwestern Oregon and California.

Range in PNW: Throughout, except Columbia Basin

Habitat: Forests and meadows

Host plants: Species of violet (*Viola*), including *V. adunca*

The two photos (below) of a pair of butterflies in copulation, taken in the Wenatchee Mountains of Washington, show Zerene's heavy black markings on top and large silver spots on the underside. Zerene Fritillary is a widespread species with a high degree of variation in different geographic regions. One variety, a subspecies named *Speyeria zerene hippolyta* or Oregon Silverspot (opposite, top), inhabits only grassy hills overlooking the Pacific Ocean. This habitat is being gobbled up by humans for houses and, due mainly to a fire suppression policy, is being invaded by brushy plants. The Oregon Silverspot's continued existence is tenuous, and it is on the federal endangered species list. The Oregon Silverspot is not as large as other Zerenes, has smaller silver spots, and has a narrow but bright yellow-orange submarginal band that contrasts prominently with the darker basal area of the hindwing.

DOUG HEPBURN

DOUG HEPBURN

WILLIAM NEILL

WILLIAM NEILL

Great Spangled Fritillary   *Speyeria cybele*

A.k.a., Leto Fritillary, *S. leto*

Wingspan: 2½–2¾ inches

Description: In males, the **top** is bright orange-brown with black marks that are reduced toward the outer wing borders; in females, the top is two-toned: dark brown in the basal half and yellow in the outer half. The **underside** of the hindwing is brown with a wide yellow submarginal band. The spots are silver, small, and sparse.

Range in PNW: Throughout, except Columbia Basin

Habitat: Forests and meadows

Host plants: Species of violet (*Viola*), including *V. glabella*

You can recognize Great Spangled Fritillary males (bottom left and right) by their bright color and small silver spots. It's unlikely you will confuse the striking females (top), with their two-toned wings, with any other fritillary in the area. If you start up the footpath to the top of Lookout Mountain in the Ochoco Mountains in the summer, you'll shortly come across clouds of fritillaries—Great Spangleds among them—feeding on mint near the old mine. Watch for these unique females.

DOUG HEPBURN

WILLIAM NEILL

DOUG HEPBURN

Coronis Fritillary   *Speyeria coronis*

Wingspan: 2¼–2¾ inches

Description: The **top** is orange-brown with black marks. The **underside** of the hindwing is pale brown or greenish brown with a distinct submarginal ochre band; the spots are silver, large, and rimmed by a fine dark line, and the silver spots in the submarginal row are usually flattened into ovals, especially near the anal angle.

Range in PNW: Cascade Mountains extending into California, and mountains in eastern Oregon

Habitat: Arid mountains and hillsides

Host plants: Species of violet (*Viola*), including *V. beckwithii*

Coronis Fritillary and Zerene Fritillary can be difficult to tell apart, but Coronis tends to be bigger and brighter. Coronis is one of the earliest fritillaries on the wing—in June or even May at Satus Pass, Washington, and in the Deschutes River canyon in Oregon; and in July, at higher elevations in Oregon's Ochoco, Elkhorn, and Steens Mountains.

WILLIAM NEILL

WILLIAM NEILL

WILLIAM NEILL

Mormon Fritillary *Speyeria mormonia*

Wingspan: 1¾–1⅞ inches

Description: The forewings are rounded. The **top** is orange-brown or yellow-brown with delicate black marks. The **underside** of the hindwing is ochre, usually smeared with green, and has a wide, paler submarginal band; the spots are small and elongated and are either silver or ochre.

Range in PNW: Cascade Mountains eastward

Habitat: Mountain meadows and alpine areas

Host plants: Species of violet (*Viola*), including *V. palustris*

Compared to other *Speyeria* species, the Mormon Fritillary is smaller, and because of the scantier amount of black, it's brighter. The two butterflies pictured here on aster blossoms are males in the Ochoco Mountains. The other Mormon Fritillary shown, a female at Tiffany Meadows in the Okanogan Highlands, has heavier black markings. Hikers often see these butterflies in high mountain meadows. I remember enjoying them at Louden Lake, 7,000 feet up in the Okanogan Highlands, a long day's trek from the Iron Gate trailhead. A more convenient place to see them is in the meadows of Marks Creek alongside U.S. 26 in the Ochoco Mountains.

DOUG HEPBURN

DOUG HEPBURN

Western Meadow Fritillary *Boloria epithore*
A.k.a., Pacific Fritillary

Wingspan: 1⅜–1⅝ inches

Description: The **top** is orange-brown with black marks. The **underside** of the hindwing has a transverse band of yellow patches in the basal area, and the outer half is violet and ochre. The wings are rounded.

Range in PNW: Cascade Mountains westward, and northeastern Washington and Oregon into Idaho

Habitat: Meadows

Host plants: Species of violet (*Viola*), including *V. glabella*

Butterflies in the genus *Boloria*, if viewed from above, look like miniature versions of *Speyeria* species and are sometimes referred to as lesser fritillaries. The main features that distinguish the various species of *Boloria* occur on the underside of the hindwing. In the Pacific Northwest, the most common species of this genus is the Western Meadow Fritillary. Its preferred home is the Cascade Mountains and Coast Range, where it flies from May to early July in forest openings and on sunny hillsides.

DOUG HEPBURN

Arctic Fritillary   *Boloria chariclea*

A.k.a., *B. titania*

Wingspan: 1⅜–1⅝ inches

Description: The **top** is orange-brown with black marks, which are heavier in females. The **underside** of the hindwing is purplish brown with a transverse band of angular yellow blotches.

Range in PNW: Cascade and Olympic Mountains in Washington, extending northward into Canada

Habitat: Montane meadows

Host plants: Species of willow (*Salix*) and violet (*Viola*)

The Arctic Fritillary, widely distributed in the subarctic, occurs in this area in the high meadows on Mount Adams and Mount Rainier and in the Olympics and North Cascades. Two of these photographs show the top surface of the butterfly; in one (left), a male sucks nectar from a yellow composite blossom, and in the other (bottom right), we see a female's abdomen plump with eggs. Note the female's dark wing borders. The distinctive markings are on the underside of the hindwing, as illustrated in the photograph of the male on the aster blossom.

DOUG HEPBURN

WILLIAM NEILL

DOUG HEPBURN

Astarte Fritillary *Boloria astarte*

Wingspan: 1⅝–1⅞ inches

Description: The **top** is dingy yellow-orange with black marks. The **underside** of the hindwing is pale orange with a transverse, irregular buff band; the outer half is paler with a row of black dots.

Range in PNW: North Cascades

Habitat: Alpine areas

Host plant: Spotted saxifrage (*Saxifraga bronchialis*)

A truly alpine resident, the Astarte Fritillary is at home on windswept rocky ledges of Washington's North Cascades near the Canadian border. Astartes alight to rest only reluctantly, rising up again to disappear in the wind at the slightest provocation, so you'll need patience to get close enough for a good look. The bare ground and lichen-covered rock in the photographs showcase the butterfly's habitat. Its life cycle takes two years, and adults fly only in even-numbered years.

Silver-bordered Fritillary   *Boloria selene*

Wingspan: 1⅜–1½ inches

Description: The **top** is bright orange-brown with dark marks and dark outer margins. The **underside** of the hindwing is brown and yellow, sprinkled with numerous silver spots.

Range in PNW: Eastern Washington into Idaho and Canada, and isolated sites in eastern Oregon

Habitat: Wet meadows

Host plants: Species of violet (*Viola*), including *V. palustris* and *V. nephrophylla*

The Silver-bordered Fritillary is the only *Boloria* species with silver spots. The butterfly showing its underside spots (bottom left) is in copulation; its mate is oriented on edge so that its narrow profile is scarcely visible. The caterpillar has a pair of thin black appendages attached near its head. Mainly a Canadian and Rocky Mountain resident, the Silver-bordered Fritillary is limited in the Pacific Northwest to a few isolated colonies situated in marshes.

CHECKERSPOTS

Anicia Checkerspot   *Euphydryas anicia*
A.k.a., Variable Checkerspot

Wingspan: 1⅜–1⅞ inches

Description: The **top** is spotted black, red, and buff. The **underside** is brick red and buff. Variation in features is common from one individual to the next.

Range in PNW: East of Cascade Mountains

Habitat: Arid prairies and rock outcroppings

Host plants: Species of paintbrush (*Castilleja*) and *Penstemon*

The photographs here of the Anicia Checkerspot caterpillar grazing on penstemon leaves and the Anicia butterfly with a yellow flower under its hindwings were taken at the edge of the Alvord Desert in southeastern Oregon. The other butterfly pictured is a smaller, darker variety of Anicia Checkerspot that occurs in the mountains of northern Washington. Yet another variety in the high desert, not shown, is almost wholly black and white. Adults fly in midspring in the Oregon desert and in early summer in the cooler mountains of Washington.

WILLIAM NEILL

DOUG HEPBURN

WILLIAM NEILL

Snowberry Checkerspot   *Euphydryas chalcedona*

A.k.a., Variable Checkerspot

Wingspan: 1½–2 inches

Description: The **top** is mostly black, with buff spots, red wing borders, and a few red spots. The **underside** is brick red and buff. The forewings are long.

Range in PNW: Throughout

Habitat: Open mountain slopes

Host plants: Species of snowberry (*Symphoricarpos*) and *Penstemon*

This is the largest and darkest checkerspot, as well as the most common. Some individuals have more red markings on the top side of the wings than the one pictured here on a daisy. Frequently, you'll see them sitting on dirt roads through open woods, where they rise up as your car rumbles by. As with the other checkerspots, the eggs are laid in clusters and the caterpillars feed together for the first few weeks. They hibernate in a group when partially grown. Pupae of checkerspots are suspended head down. In the photograph here, the discarded black caterpillar skin still clings to the end of the pupa.

DOUG HEPBURN

DOUG HEPBURN

WILLIAM NEILL

WILLIAM NEILL

Edith's Checkerspot   *Euphydryas editha*

Wingspan: 1⅜–1⅝ inches

Description: The **top** is spotted black, red, and buff. The **underside** is brick red and buff. The wings typically are rounded.

Range in PNW: Throughout

Habitat: Mountain meadows

Host plants: Species of plantain (*Plantago*)

Rounded wings help identify Edith's Checkerspot, although the shape varies among individuals. The top usually is redder than in its relatives, and the edges between the square spots are not quite so sharply drawn. If you examine the photo of the underside of the Snowberry Checkerspot (page 124, top left), you can see a whitish buff band bordered by black lines crossing the center of the hindwing. Some of the buff color leaks past the black line, spilling into the red area toward the outer margin of the wing. This effect also occurs in the Anicia Checkerspot, but not in Edith's, whose buff band stays within its black borders, as seen here. This feature is considered crucial for distinguishing Edith's Checkerspot from other Checkerspots. If you walk up the Iron Mountain wildflower trail in Oregon's central Cascades in July, you're likely to see Edith's Checkerspots on the open rocky slope within sight of the fire tower.

WILLIAM NEILL

WILLIAM NEILL

Leanira Checkerspot   *Thessalia leanira*

Wingspan: 1⅝–1¾ inches

Description: The **top** is either brown with yellow spots (forest variety) or orange with wing veins outlined in black (desert variety). The **underside** of the hindwing is buff with black wing vein lines and a transverse black band containing buff spots. The body has black and buff bands.

Range in PNW: Southern Oregon southward into California

Habitat: Sagebrush flats and open forests

Host plants: Species of paintbrush (*Castilleja*)

Two very different subspecies of Leanira Checkerspot occur in Oregon: a dark variety in the forested Siskiyou Mountains and a light form in the southeastern desert basin. The top of the forest dweller is shown opposite bottom left). The other adults shown, photographed at the edge of the barren Alvord Desert in southeastern Oregon, are the desert variety. For a brief period in the spring, wildflowers cover the sandy ground of this terrain and provide nectar for newly emerged butterflies. During May, female Leanira Checkerspots deposit clumps of eggs on paintbrush growing in the shade of sagebrush. Caterpillars hatch from the eggs and begin to feed. By June, the sun is blistering and most wildflowers wither. Young checkerspot caterpillars begin their diapause then, remaining inactive and out of sight through the summer, fall, and winter. In April, when fresh stems of paintbrush regenerate, caterpillars awaken and resume feeding. The caterpillar shown here is older, photographed in late April. The pupa, photographed in May, blends with the dead gray sagebrush twigs. An adult will hatch from it in two weeks, and the cycle will repeat.

WILLIAM NEILL

WILLIAM NEILL

WILLIAM NEILL

DOUG HEPBURN

WILLIAM NEILL

Checkerspots 127

Northern Checkerspot   *Chlosyne palla*

Wingspan: 1⅜–1⅝ inches

Description: In males, the **top** is spotted brown and orange; in females, the top is darker, often black, with buff spots. The **underside** of the hindwing is dull orange with transverse bands of pale squares.

Range in PNW: Siskiyou and Cascade Mountains eastward

Habitat: Prairies, canyons, and open forests

Host plants: Species of *Aster*

The Northern Checkerspot is a common species. Like many other checkerspots, populations of the Northern Checkerspot in different geographic areas often look a little different from each other. The photo here showing the upper surface was taken in central Oregon in May. The other picture, from the Klamath River canyon in northern California, demonstrates the checkered pattern of white and orange squares on the underside.

CRESCENTS

Mylitta Crescent   *Phyciodes mylitta*

Wingspan: 1⅛–1⅜ inches

Description: The **top** is orange with black marks, which are heavier in females. A broad transverse band across the wings is devoid of black marks; this band is lighter and more yellow in females. The **underside** of the hindwing is checkered brown, yellow, and ochre. (A submarginal pale, crescent-shaped spot is present on the underside of the hindwing in all crescent butterflies.)

Range in PNW: Throughout

Habitat: Many

Host plants: Many species of thistle (various genuses)

The common Mylitta Crescent occurs from sea level to high mountain meadows. Undaunted by urban sprawl, the black spiny caterpillars thrive on the thistle that flourishes in vacant lots and unattended fields. Eggs are deposited in clusters, and the young caterpillars remain together. The photographs show a female on a purple aster, a male on a white daisy, and a group of newborn caterpillars.

Field Crescent   *Phyciodes pulchellus*

A.k.a., *P. pulchella, P. pratensis, P. campestris*

Wingspan: 1 ¼–1 ½ inches

Description: The **top** is dark brown with transverse brown and ochre bands, which are much reduced in males. The outer margin of the forewing is rounded. The **underside** of the hindwing is mostly yellow-orange in males and is checkered brown and ochre in females.

Range in PNW: Throughout

Habitat: Mountain meadows and fields

Host plants: Species of *Aster*

Male Field Crescents are dark on top and bright on the underside (below). The females (opposite) have a more checkered pattern on both the top and the underside. I watched a female Field Crescent place her pearly eggs in neat parallel rows on the surface of an aster leaf. It took her several minutes to complete this mosaic of about a hundred eggs. The newborn caterpillars make a communal nest, bringing leaves together with threads of silk. They eat the leaves at the edge of the nest. Later, when they are as developed as the one shown here, the caterpillars disperse to forage singly.

WILLIAM NEILL

WILLIAM NEILL

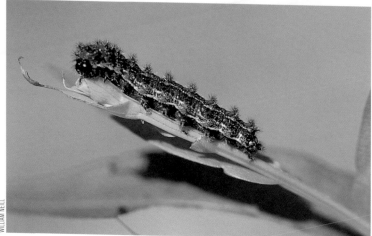

WILLIAM NEILL

Pale Crescent   *Phyciodes pallidus*

A.k.a., *P. pallida*

Wingspan: 1½–1¾ inches

Description: The **top** is orange with black marks, including a large black splotch on the trailing edge of the forewing; females also have pale transverse bands. In males, the **underside** is yellow or ochre and faintly checkered; in females, it is ochre and brown and prominently checkered. The outer margin of the forewing is slightly concave.

Range in PNW: Scattered sites east of Cascade Mountains

Habitat: Hot arid canyons

Host plants: Species of thistle (various genuses), including wavy-leaf thistle (*Cirsium undulatum*)

The Pale Crescent looks much like a large version of the Mylitta Crescent. The conspicuous large black mark centered on the trailing edge of the forewing is a consistent distinguishing mark. The Pale Crescent is an uncommon butterfly with a rather narrow flight period, mainly May. This male (left) was taking nectar from gaillardia growing on a gravel slope that rises toward the cliffs of the Deschutes River canyon. A female is also shown.

WILLIAM NEILL

ANGLEWINGS and THEIR RELATIVES

Satyr Anglewing *Polygonia satyrus*
A.k.a., Satyr Comma

Wingspan: 1¾–2 inches

Description: The **top** is orange-brown with dark brown spots and irregular outer wing margins. The **underside** is warm brown, mottled, and transversely striped, with less contrast in females; the hindwing has a silver comma.

Range in PNW: Throughout

Habitat: Streamsides and moist woods

Host plant: Stinging nettle (*Urtica dioica*)

This is the region's only *Polygonia* species with a warm brown underside. The pictures show the top of a female (on foliage) and the underside of a male (on bark). Eggs are fastened to the underside edge of nettle leaves. Caterpillars hide beneath the leaves, sometimes drawing the leaves downward with silk threads. This may conceal them from predators but can make them easier for us to locate. You can find this species anywhere nettle grows, especially near streams in mountain foothills. In the Portland area, check nettle plants at Oaks Bottom, at Tryon Creek State Park, and along the Portland Audubon Nature Trail.

DOGU HEPBURN

WILLIAM NEILL

WILLIAM NEILL

Hoary Comma *Polygonia gracilis*

A.k.a., Hoary Anglewing, Zephyr Anglewing, *P. zephyrus*

Wingspan: 1¾–2 inches

Description: The **top** is orange-brown with dark brown spots and irregular outer wing margins. The **underside** is warm mottled gray, and the lighter outer half contains vague yellow spots; the hindwing has a silver comma.

Range in PNW: Cascade Mountains eastward and Olympic Mountains

Habitat: Forests and montane meadows

Host plants: Species of currant (*Ribes*), including *R. cereum*, *R. aureum*, and *R. viscosissimum*

While the top of the Hoary Comma resembles the Satyr Anglewing, its underside is gray rather than brown. Hoary Commas are a delight to see on fading aster blooms when summer is winding down in the high mountain meadows. Look for them near the parking lots at the alpine lodges on Mount Hood and Mount Rainier. The Hoary Comma caterpillar, shown here on a sticky currant plant, has elaborate branched spines, is orange at the anterior end of the body and white posteriorly, and has a white stripe down its back.

WILLIAM NEILL

Green Comma *Polygonia faunus*

A.k.a., Faun Anglewing

Wingspan: 1⅝–2 inches

Description: The **top** is orange-brown with dark brown spots and wing borders and ragged outer wing margins. The **underside** is mottled dark gray-brown with vague green spots; the hindwing has a silver comma.

Range in PNW: Cascade Mountains westward and northeast Oregon northward into Washington and Canada and eastward into Idaho

Habitat: Streamsides and moist woods

Host plants: Alder trees (*Alnus*)

The Green Comma is a small anglewing, darker than the Hoary Comma and the Satyr Anglewing, and with especially ragged wing margins. The small green spots on the underside, visible in the photograph, are a unique feature and are clearest on fresh individuals. I've watched these anglewings imbibing sap from willow and alder branches and juice oozing from rotting fruit.

WILLIAM NEILL

WILLIAM NEILL

Oreas Anglewing   *Polygonia oreas*

A.k.a., Oreas Comma, Dark Anglewing, *P. progne*

Wingspan: 1⅞–2 inches

Description: The orange-brown **top** has dark brown spots and dark brown outer borders. The outer wing margins are irregular. The **underside** is mottled very dark gray-brown, with a less distinct pattern in females; the hindwing has a silver comma.

Range in PNW: Cascade Mountains westward and northeast Oregon into Idaho

Habitat: Streamsides and moist woods

Host plants: Species of currant (*Ribes*), including *R. divaricatum*

The Oreas Anglewing can usually be identified by its very dark underside. Although this butterfly is scarce, it often shows up in autumn in the Oregon Coast Range, sunning on dirt roads along the Nestucca River and Mill Creek. In April, I watched a female laying eggs on straggly gooseberry bushes overhanging the Metolius River. The ringed, spiny body of the caterpillar is bronzed near the head.

WILLIAM NEILL   WILLIAM NEILL

California Tortoiseshell   *Nymphalis californica*

Wingspan: 1⅞–2⅛ inches

Description: The **top** is brownish orange with a dark brown outer border. There are a few large brown spots on the forewing and one on the hindwing, and there is a small white patch near the forewing apex. The wing margins are irregular. The **underside** is mottled dark brown.

Range in PNW: Throughout

Habitat: Open forests and mountains

Host plants: Species of *Ceanothus*

Compared to the anglewings and commas (*Polygonia*), the California Tortoiseshell is slightly larger, has fewer dark spots, and has a bit of white near the tip of the forewing. There is no silver comma. This tortoiseshell's population fluctuates widely; when they are abundant, masses of adults congregate and travel together, perhaps to locate new breeding sites. Motorists often notice crowds of them crossing the highway and spattering against the windshield. The spiny caterpillars, when numerous, can defoliate ceanothus bushes. The pupa hangs head down from a single silk attachment.

DOUG HEPBURN

WILLIAM NEILL

WILLIAM NEILL

Milbert's Tortoiseshell   *Nymphalis milberti*

Wingspan: 1⅝–2 inches

Description: The **top** is dark brown with a bright yellow and orange transverse band across all of the wings. The outer wing margins are irregular. The **underside** is gray-brown, with a lighter outer half.

Range in PNW: Throughout

Habitat: Mountain meadows and streamsides

Host plant: Stinging nettle (*Urtica dioica*)

It's easy to recognize the brightly colored band across the upper side of the wings of Milbert's Tortoiseshell. This is one of the most common butterflies in high mountain meadows, where hikers are certain to notice it. Milbert's Tortoiseshell avidly feeds on composite flowers along trails and in meadows, pausing with wings open and colors displayed, like the one here resting on nettle. In flight, it appears dark. Pale green eggs are laid in clusters on the underside of nettle leaves. Look for the spiny black caterpillars on plants with ragged, partially eaten leaves. The caterpillars stay in groups for a few weeks, then feed singly. The pupae are bronze-colored.

Mourning Cloak   *Nymphalis antiopa*

Wingspan: 2⅜–2⅝ inches

Description: The **top** is brownish purple with bright blue submarginal spots and a cream outer border. The outer wing margins are irregular. The **underside** is dark with a cream outer border.

Range in PNW: Throughout

Habitat: Streamsides and forests

Host plants: Species of willow (*Salix*), and occasionally other trees

In the Pacific Northwest, the Mourning Cloak is the only large dark butterfly with pale borders. The female commits many of her eggs, or even her whole supply, to one location, arranging them in a geometric mosaic encircling a willow twig. This clutch pictured amounted to 240 eggs, most of them purple and a few yellow. Infant caterpillars cling together on the empty eggshells, trailing silk strands to guide them home from feeding forays. When disturbed, they snap their bodies outward in unison, creating the illusion of a single formidable animal. Mature caterpillars forage alone. Pupae hang head down. The species produces two broods and hibernates as adults.

ARISTOCRATS _____

A Monarch, a Viceroy, Admirals, Ladies, and a Sister

A fanciful, tongue-in-cheek term? The term may be fanciful, but the grouping itself is useful in field identification. These butterflies all share easily recognizable physical features: they're big, bright, and bold. With the exception of the Monarch, they are also closely related. Looking over the common names of the butterflies in this assemblage, I found the collective term *Aristocrats* irresistible. Buckeye is more of a commoner, but where would aristocrats be without commoners?

Monarch   *Danaus plexippus*

Wingspan: 3½–3¾ inches

Description: The **top** is orange with black wing veins and a black border containing white spots. The female is darker. In males, the black line in the center of the hindwing has an oval enlargement. The forewing is long and pointed.

Range in PNW: Throughout

Habitat: Open areas, including prairies and farms

Host plants: Species of milkweed (*Asclepias*), including *A. speciosa* and *A. fascicularis*

The Monarch is a transient summer resident of the Northwest. While most butterflies cope with the full cycle of seasons that comes with their breeding place, the Monarch flies far to the south to survive the winter. Adults that reach their winter destinations in Southern California (western population) or central Mexico (mainly the population east of the Continental Divide) live through the winter in huge colonies. In early spring, they begin their long return. Successive broods move northward, rearing their young on milkweed along the way, eventually reaching Canada before the cool autumn turns them back once more. The generation that flies south to the winter encampment knows the way somehow, even though they have never been there. This procedure has been going on for a long time—probably thousands of years.

Monarch caterpillars retain toxic alkaloids from the milkweed they eat, and the caterpillars, pupae, and adults all make birds sick when eaten. The bright, recognizable coloring of each of these stages in the life cycle helps remind birds of the consequences of eating a Monarch (something used to the advantage of another species as well—see the Viceroy account). Monarchs are common in some places, especially in the midwestern United States, but are only thinly scattered across Oregon and Washington.

DOUG HEPBURN

WILLIAM NEILL

WILLIAM NEILL

Viceroy   *Limenitis archippus*

Wingspan: 2¼–2⅝ inches

Description: The **top** is orange with black wing veins and a black border containing white spots. A curved transverse black line crosses the veins on the hindwing.

Range in PNW: East of the Cascade Mountains in the Columbia and Snake River basins

Habitat: Streamsides

Host plants: Species of willow (*Salix*)

Although not closely related, the Viceroy mimics the Monarch. Apparently, in its world, impersonating a king is a profitable ploy without much attendant risk. Birds avoid the perfectly digestible Viceroy, mistaking it for a Monarch, which they have learned makes them sick. The Viceroy's mimicry is credited to a chance mutation that was convincing enough to birds to favor the aberrant form's survival. To reach the degree of similarity we now see, the resemblance must have been refined by further improvements that enhanced survival over successive generations. The Viceroy is not as large as the Monarch and has a single curved black line that crosses the other black lines on the hindwing. The Viceroy is scarce in the Pacific Northwest, limited mainly to willow thickets along the Columbia River and its tributaries. Perhaps the paucity of its look-alike, the Monarch, in the same area figures in its scarcity—after all, mimicry only works when the real thing is common enough to condition predators. The Viceroy caterpillar in the photo, small and dark with a white saddle, is entering its hibernaculum (hibernation shelter) headfirst, perhaps to apply some finishing touches. Like the Lorquin's Admiral, for hibernation it will turn around so that its head capsule blocks the entrance. Mature caterpillars (bottom left) can be mottled green or brown.

WILLIAM NEILL

WILLIAM NEILL

WILLIAM NEILL

Lorquin's Admiral   *Limenitis lorquini*

Wingspan: 2–2¼ inches

Description: The **top** is very dark brown with a transverse white band and an orange forewing apex. The **underside** is similar but lighter.

Range in PNW: Throughout

Habitat: Streamsides

Host plants: Species of willow (*Salix*)

Lorquin's Admiral is usually found near water, perched on a bush or drinking from moist ground. Its flight is distinctive, with successive bursts of rapid flapping alternating with gliding on horizontally positioned wings. The species has two broods. For the summer brood, females deposit their eggs on willows in June. The green egg is shaped like an acorn missing its cap and has facets that reflect sunlight. The newborn caterpillar (opposite, top) crawls to the tip of the leaf. There, it begins to eat away the substance of the leaf on both sides of the midvein, stripping it into a terminal spur where the caterpillar can rest, facing outward. To feed, the infant caterpillar turns itself around dexterously on its high-wire perch and nibbles away at the leaf, effectively lengthening its spur. Securing itself further from ants and other unwelcome neighbors, the caterpillar attaches a bulky bundle of leaf remnants and feces on the terminal spur (visible at center in the photo of the infant) as a bulwark against intruders, relocating the bundle as needed. In just a few weeks, the caterpillar outgrows this arrangement and travels about the willow bush to forage. Larger Lorquin's Admiral caterpillars (opposite, bottom right) are adorned garishly with warts and menacing horns, and the pupa is also extravagantly ornamented.

DOUG HEPBURN

WILLIAM NEILL

The second brood hibernates as immature caterpillars (see Viceroy species account, page 142). In the fall, a small caterpillar curls the proximal portion of its partly eaten leaf into a tube after reinforcing its stem attachment with silk. The distal end of the tube is left open and the midvein spur serves as a threshold. The caterpillar wriggles in backwards, positioning its hard head capsule to block the entrance. The caterpillar stays in its snug hut, called a hibernaculum, until the next spring.

Red Admiral   *Vanessa atalanta*

A.k.a., Red Admirable

> **Wingspan:** 1⅞–2⅛ inches
>
> **Description:** The **top** is very dark brown with diagonal red bands, one across the forewing and the other at the outer border of the hindwing. The apex of the forewing has white spots.
>
> **Range in PNW:** Throughout
>
> **Habitat:** Streamsides and woods
>
> **Host plant:** Stinging nettle (*Urtica dioica*)

The red bands and white spots are easily recognized field marks for the Red Admiral. The photos on the next page (clockwise from top left) show the sequence of the Red Admiral's early development. In May, females emerge from hibernation and attach eggs to young nettle leaves, usually near the top of the plant. The egg is bright green and resembles a miniature ribbed barrel. The caterpillar that hatches makes a shelter from a small leaf, approximating the edges with a lacework of silk. As the caterpillar grows, it constructs new, larger nests. The fully grown caterpillar is black and white. Before pupating, it pulls several leaves together and binds them with silk strands to create a room. It pupates hanging head down from the ceiling, enclosed by leaves and hidden from view. For this photo (opposite, bottom), I cut away the leaves forming one wall to photograph the pupa suspended within. A few lengths of silk fixing the leaves in position can still be seen.

WILLIAM NEILL

DOUG HEPBURN

WILLIAM NEILL

WILLIAM NEILL

Painted Lady   *Vanessa cardui*

Wingspan: 1⅞–2⅛ inches

Description: The **top** is orange and black with a black area on the apex of the forewing that contains white spots and a white rectangle; the hindwing has a submarginal row of four dark spots, some with blue centers. The **underside** of the hindwing is mottled and has a submarginal row of four small eyespots.

Range in PNW: Throughout

Habitat: Open areas

Host plants: Species of thistle (various genuses) and lupine (*Lupinus*), and others

The Painted Lady can be distinguished from the West Coast Lady by the white rectangular patch within the black apex area of the forewing (orange in the West Coast Lady) and from the American Lady by the difference in the spots on the underside of the hindwing. In all three of the ladies, the veins on the underside of the hindwing are outlined by fine white lines, looking a bit like a spiderweb (perhaps that's not a coincidence). The abundance of the Painted Lady population varies greatly from year to year. The spiny caterpillars feed on thistle, among other plants, and construct loose silk nests.

West Coast Lady *Vanessa annabella*

Wingspan: 1¾–1⅞ inches

Description: The forewing apex is squared. The **top** is orange and black, and the black apex of the forewing contains white spots and an orange rectangle. The hindwing has a submarginal row of four small eyespots with blue centers. The **underside** of the hindwing is mottled and has a submarginal row of four small eyespots.

Range in PNW: Throughout

Habitat: Open areas and mountain meadows

Host plants: Species of mallow (*Malva*)

You can distinguish the West Coast Lady from the Painted Lady by its square forewing tip and the orange color of the forewing rectangle. To tell the West Coast Lady from the American Lady, look for the West Coast's square forewing tip and the row of spots on the underside of the hindwing, multiple and small. The West Coast Lady is at home in mountain meadows, forest openings, streamsides, and suburban gardens. I've come across them feeding on flowers at the end of the summer in high places like the Wenatchee Mountains, near the summit of Strawberry Mountain, and at the Mount Hood Meadows ski lodge. I remember watching one basking in a patch of sunlight in my Portland garden on a fine day well into November.

DOUG HEPBURN

American Lady *Vanessa virginiensis*
A.k.a., American Painted Lady

Wingspan: 1⅞–2⅛ inches

Description: The outer margin of the forewing is concave. The **top** is orange and black, and the black apex of the forewing contains white spots and a white or orange rectangle. The hindwing has a submarginal row of four small eyespots with blue centers. The **underside** of the hindwing has linear streaks and two very large, ringed eyespots.

Range in PNW: Southern Washington southward into California

Habitat: Meadows and open weedy areas

Host plants: Pearly everlasting (*Anaphalis margaritacea*) and others

The American Lady can be distinguished from the other two ladies by the two large eyespots on the underside of its hindwing. Its banded, spiny caterpillar is shown here on its host plant. Before pupating, a caterpillar I watched pulled leaves of the pearly everlasting plant slightly downward to veil its whereabouts—yet not so drastically as to call unwanted attention—and fixed them there with silk strands. With the "curtains" drawn in this way, the pupa is hard to see.

On the eve of dispatching this manuscript to the publisher, I stumbled on a drawing of the American Lady pupa in W. J. Holland's 1901 classic, *The Butterfly Book*. The butterfly was then called Hunter's Butterfly (*Pyrameis huntera*). There was the pupa hanging down, shielded by silk and pearly everlasting leaves—a precise replica of our photo. At first the similarity of the two images startled me, yet it shouldn't have. That is exactly how butterflies function: adhering to fixed patterns of behavior, with no change from one century to the next, or the next.

WILLIAM NEILL

WILLIAM NEILL

WILLIAM NEILL

WILLIAM NEILL

California Sister   *Adelpha bredowii*

Wingspan: 2⅛–2⅝ inches

Description: The **top** is very dark brown with a transverse white band and a large round orange patch near the forewing apex. The **underside** is lighter and has narrow clear blue bands and spots around the perimeter of the wings.

Range in PNW: Western Oregon southward into California

Habitat: Deciduous forests and streamsides

Host plants: Species of oak (*Quercus*)

The pattern on the California Sister's top bears some resemblance to Lorquin's Admiral, but the orange patch is bigger and doesn't reach the wing tip, and the white band is narrower. The beautiful, delicate blue on the underside of the California Sister is a definitive field mark. The butterfly's habitat is forests with oak trees. Adults fly up among the branches but eventually come down to drink at mud. The big caterpillars of the species are mottled green with warts and horns.

Common Buckeye   *Junonia coenia*

A.k.a., Buckeye

Wingspan: 1⅝–1⅞ inches

Description: The brown **top** has three large false eyespots and a buff patch on the forewing. The **underside** is tan and rather plain except for a forewing eyespot.

Range in PNW: Southern Oregon southward into California

Habitat: Open areas

Host plants: Species of plantain (*Plantago*), *Penstemon*, and paintbrush (*Castilleja*)

When the Common Buckeye sits still, you'll easily recognize it by the false eyespots. This is a restless, pugnacious butterfly that chases after insects and anything else that comes into its view. In flight, it's a dark blur. A favorite haunt is weedy old fields crossed by dirt roads, where males sit in the sun. Common in the American South, the Buckeye enters only the southern portion of the Pacific Northwest. Its spiny caterpillar is dark on top with lighter lateral lines.

DOUG HEPBURN

Ochre Ringlet *Coenonympha tullia*
A.k.a., Common Ringlet

Wingspan: 1–1½ inches

Description: The **top** is ochre. On the **underside**, the forewing is orange or ochre, and most individuals east of the Cascades have a small eyespot near the apex. The hindwing is gray-brown, marked with a pale scalloped band.

Range in PNW: Throughout

Habitat: Prairies and meadows

Host plants: Species of grass (various genera)

At home in lawns as well as native grasslands, Ochre Ringlets are perhaps the most numerous butterflies in the Pacific Northwest. During the past few decades they have extended their range into the northeastern United States, possibly by breeding along freeways. Ringlets living west of the Cascades (top left) are plain except for the pale scalloped figure on the underside. Those east of the Cascades (top right) usually have a forewing eyespot, and in southern Oregon and California, they're bleached out with minimal markings. With multiple broods, they're with us summer and spring, flying low to the ground in a lazy bobbing motion. Translucent eggs are stuck to the side of a blade of grass. The caterpillar and pupa, striped to blend with grass stalks, can be either green or brown. Sometimes the pupa surrounds itself with blades of grass gathered together by a few silk threads.

DOUG HEPBURN

DOUG HEPBURN

WILLIAM NEILL

WILLIAM NEILL

Common Wood Nymph   *Cercyonis pegala*

A.k.a., Large Wood Nymph

Wingspan: 1¾–2⅛ inches

Description: The **top** is brown, and the forewing has two dark spots, sometimes with pupils. The **underside** is gray-brown with fine striations. The forewing has two prominent eyespots with white or pale blue pupils encircled by black and yellow rings; the eyespot closest to the apex is usually smaller than the other, never larger.

Range in PNW: Throughout

Habitat: Open forests and prairies

Host plants: Species of grass (various genera)

The three wood nymphs look a lot alike, so check out the other two *Cercyonis* species. *C. Pegala*, the Common Wood Nymph, is a variable species. In desert populations, the eyespots may be surrounded by an extensive yellow area on both surfaces of the forewing, especially in females. The camouflage pattern of the mating pair in the picture (female on the right) blends with the ponderosa pine bark on which they rest. Larvae that hatch from the eggs will enter diapause and remain dormant until the next spring, when they will awaken to feed on fresh grass shoots. Adults emerge in summer.

DOUG HEPBURN

Dark Wood Nymph   *Cercyonis oetus*

A.k.a., Small Wood Nymph

Wingspan: 1½–1⅞ inches

Description: The **top** is grayish brown, and the forewing has two dark spots. The **underside** is gray-brown with fine striations. The hindwing has a dark transverse zigzag line, and the forewing has two prominent eyespots with pale pupils encircled by black and yellow rings; the eyespot closest to the apex is larger than the other.

Range in PNW: Cascade Mountains eastward

Habitat: Open forests and prairies

Host plants: Species of grass (various genera)

The Dark Wood Nymph is a denizen of the open prairie and its wooded fringes, staying close to scruffy bushes into which it seems to vanish when alarmed. The most reliable features for discriminating between Dark and Common Wood Nymphs are the pair of forewing eyespots and the transverse line across the center of the hindwing. In the Dark Wood Nymph, the eyespot nearest the wing apex is the larger one. The transverse line, wavy in the Common Wood Nymph, is deeply zigzagged with sharp points in the Dark Wood Nymph. There is one brood, and it flies from June through August. The Dark Wood Nymph likes flowers.

DOUG HEPBURN

Great Basin Wood Nymph   *Cercyonis sthenele*

Wingspan: 1½–1¾ inches

Description: The **top** is grayish brown, and the forewing has two dark spots. The **underside** is gray-brown with fine striations. The hindwing has a dark transverse line, the center of which bulges toward the outer margin, and the outer half of the hindwing is frosted with white scales. The forewing has two prominent eyespots with pale pupils encircled by black and yellow rings; the eyespot closest to the apex is usually larger than the other, never smaller.

Range in PNW: East of Cascade Mountains and southwest Oregon

Habitat: Grassland prairies

Host plants: Species of grass (various genera)

It's not always easy to tell the three wood nymphs apart, and on the sagebrush prairie, all three species may be jostling for space and nectar at the same rabbitbrush. Of the three species, the Great Basin Wood Nymph is the most consistent in appearance, and the following pointers should help to distinguish it from the others. The Great Basin Wood Nymph is usually smaller than the Common Wood Nymph, and the size of the two eyespots on the forewing relative to each other is different. In the Great Basin species, the eyespot nearer the apex is the larger of the two; in the Common Wood Nymph, it is the smaller. To rule out the Dark Wood Nymph, take note of the dark line across the hindwing. In the Dark Wood Nymph, the line is jagged; in the Great Basin species, it is smoother, with the center bulged outward like a peninsula.

WILLIAM NEILL

Common Alpine *Erebia epipsodea*
A.k.a., Butler's Alpine

Wingspan: 1 ⅛–1 ⅝ inches

Description: The **top** is brown with orange patches containing several black spots; the larger spots have a white center. On the **underside**, the forewing is brown, and the hindwing is grayish brown with black spots.

Range in PNW: Eastern Washington and northeastern Oregon

Habitat: Moist meadows

Host plants: Species of grass (various genera)

Most species of the genus *Erebia* inhabit subarctic regions. A few also occur in the Rocky Mountains, and two in the Pacific Northwest. The Common Alpine's range includes the northeastern portion of the Pacific Northwest as far south as the Ochoco Mountains. In the right habitat—wet meadows of mountain forests and high grassy prairies—it can be numerous. The Common Alpine's flight is slow, straight, and close to the ground. They're easy to catch but hard to photograph, because they don't stop often or for long. A female is shown here. Males have less orange surrounding the eyespots. Common Alpine caterpillars are laterally striped with green and light brown.

DOUG HEPBURN

Vidler's Alpine *Erebia vidleri*

Wingspan: 1½–1⅝ inches

Description: The **top** is brown. On the forewing, an orange patch shaped like the state of Vermont contains three black spots, usually with a white center. There is a smaller orange patch on the hindwing. On the brown **underside**, the forewing has the same markings as the top, but the hindwing has a curved transverse gray band and no spots.

Range in PNW: North Cascades and Olympic Mountains

Habitat: Moist alpine meadows

Host plants: Species of grass (various genera)

Vidler's Alpine is similar to the Common Alpine, but its yellow-orange patches on top are more restricted to the forewing, and the underside of the hindwing has no spots. Vidler's Alpine lives in northern Washington and southern British Columbia and nowhere else. It can be found dependably in late July or early August in the Olympic Mountains on Hurricane Ridge and in the North Cascades—for example, along the Pacific Crest Trail within sight of the Slate Peak lookout or along the Silver Lake Trail. It patrols up and down the sloping meadows, once in a while stopping at a flower, where you can get a good view, but more often dropping out of sight into the grass.

DOUG HEPBURN

DOUG HEPBURN

Ridings' Satyr   *Neominois ridingsii*

Wingspan: 1½–1¾ inches

Description: The **top** is grayish brown. Pale yellow ovals lying between the wing veins form a broad transverse band across the wings, like the fingers of a gloved hand; on the forewing, the pale band contains two white-centered black eyespots. The pattern is similar on the **underside**, but muted and speckled.

Range in PNW: Southeastern Oregon southward into Nevada

Habitat: Grassy mountaintops

Host plants: Species of grass (various genera)

Until very recently in the Pacific Northwest, Ridings' Satyr had been found only on a few grassy mountaintops in southern Oregon. Now it has also been discovered in the high desert between Bend and Burns, and further exploration of the area may turn up lots of colonies. The photos here were taken at the top of Drake's Peak in early July. When we stepped through the grass and sagebrush, satyrs would zoom ahead as gray blurs, then disappear as they sat blended with the gray backdrop. One butterfly abruptly plunged to the ground; it had been caught aloft by a robber fly and driven down by the momentum of its powerful assailant (see photo on page 18).

DOUG HEPBURN

DOUG HEPBURN

Chryxus Arctic *Oeneis chryxus*

Wingspan: 1⅞–2⅛ inches

Description: The **top** is orange-brown with a dark outer border and several black spots on the outer area of the wings; males have a dark patch extending from the base toward the apex of the forewing. The **underside** of the hindwing is stippled brown and white, with curved transverse bands.

Range in PNW: Northern Washington eastward into Idaho and northward into Canada

Habitat: Montane meadows

Host plants: Species of grass (various genera)

Most members of this genus inhabit the far north or high Rocky Mountain regions, but the range of the Chryxus Arctic reaches into the mountains of northern Washington. It rests on warm bare rocks, bleached fallen branches, or earth, where its stippled underside matches the background. Usually the Chryxus sees me before I see it, but if I follow its flight carefully, I may be able to spot where it lands. Sometimes a soundless, slow approach gets me close enough for a good look. In both *Oeneis* species that occur in this region, the males have specialized scent scales used in courtship that form a dark diagonal patch across the upper surface of the forewing.

DOUG HEPBURN

Great Arctic *Oeneis nevadensis*

A.k.a., Nevada Arctic

Wingspan: 2–2⅜ inches

Description: The outer wing margins are scalloped. The orange-brown **top** has a dark outer border, two or three eyespots on the forewing, and one eyespot on the hindwing; males have a dark patch extending from the base toward the tip of the forewing. On the **underside**, the hindwing is stippled brown and white, with curved transverse bands and a prominent pale gray patch at its leading edge.

Range in PNW: Cascade Mountains

Habitat: Forest openings

Host plants: Species of grass (various genera)

Although similar to the Chryxus Arctic, the Great Arctic is larger and brighter orange on top, and its hindwings have scalloped edges. The pale patch near the leading edge of the hindwing is the best field mark on the underside. Moreover, habitat helps distinguish the two species: the Great Arctic does not inhabit terrain any higher than foothills. It's a challenge to get close to one of these aloof butterflies as it clings to a tree trunk or branch. No matter how stealthily you inch forward, the moment your position crosses its threshold of tolerance, the butterfly explodes into flight and disappears. Females stick their eggs to blades of grass or to any nearby structure close to the ground. Young caterpillars are initially green, then turn pale brown with longitudinal stripes. They hibernate over two winters. The photo here shows a caterpillar at the end of its second summer. It will pupate the following spring. Adults are synchronized to fly together in even-numbered years.

SKIPPERS

Silver-spotted Skipper *Epargyreus clarus*

Wingspan: 1½–1¾ inches

Description: The forewing is pointed and the hindwing triangular. The **top** is brown with a translucent orange patch on the middle of the forewing. The **underside** has an orange patch on the forewing and a silver-white patch at the center of the hindwing.

Range in PNW: Cascade Mountains westward, southeastern Washington, and northeastern Oregon

Habitat: Meadows and forest openings

Host plants: Legumes, including *Lotus crassifolius*

The Silver-spotted Skipper is big, powerful, and easily recognized. It deposits eggs on the stems and leaves of its host plants in late spring. The sequence of four photographs on the next page (A–D) shows a newborn caterpillar building a shelter from a leaf of the legume *Lotus crassifolius*. In the first picture (A), the caterpillar is completing the second cut that it has chewed from the leaf margin to the midvein, freeing up a flap of leaf. The caterpillar's discarded gray eggshell is visible on the stem above. Next (B), the upper corner of the flap has been pulled toward the center of the leaf and held there by silk. The caterpillar begins to repeat this procedure with the lower corner; a single strand of silk is already in place. In the third picture (C), the flap is bent sharply over, held in position by two stout silk ropes. By the end of the day (D), the caterpillar has created a tight enclosure where it can rest and hide when not grazing. The clearance is just enough for its head to poke out. A month later, the mature caterpillar has a striped green body and a black head adorned with a pair of red spots (opposite, top right). It hibernates as either a caterpillar or a pupa, surrounded by a jumble of leaves bound together with silk.

DOUG HEPBURN

DOUG HEPBURN

WILLIAM NEILL

WILLIAM NEILL

WILLIAM NEILL

WILLIAM NEILL

WILLIAM NEILL

A

B

C

D

Skippers 165

Northern Cloudywing   *Thorybes pylades*

Wingspan: 1¼–1⅜ inches

Description: The **top** is brown with two translucent white bars at the leading edge of the forewing and another small cluster of white marks nearby. The **underside** is brown and lighter toward the outside, and the white marks on top show through.

Range in PNW: East slope of Cascade Mountains; Siskiyou Mountains; Puget Trough; other isolated sites

Habitat: Meadows in forest openings

Host plants: Species of vetch (*Vicia*), clover (*Trifolium*), and *Lotus*, and others

The Northern Cloudywing occurs across most of the United States, but its reported distribution in the Pacific Northwest is spotty. The adults are out in late spring, visiting flowers and basking. The narrow-necked, plump caterpillar makes a compact nest from its host plant's leaves.

WILLIAM NEILL

WILLIAM NEILL

Dreamy Duskywing *Erynnis icelus*

Wingspan: 1–1 ¼ inches

Description: The **top** of the forewing is bluish gray tweed in males and mottled brown in females. The hindwing is brown with rows of indistinct lighter spots. In males, the leading edge of the forewing is angled. The **underside** is brown with faint pale spots.

Range in PNW: Cascade Mountains and northeastern Oregon into Washington and Idaho

Habitat: Watercourses and openings in forests

Host plants: Species of willow (*Salix*), aspen and poplar (both *Populus*)

The Dreamy Duskywing is smaller than the Propertius Duskywing and has no translucent spots. The forewing of the male shown here (top) is bluish, whereas the female's forewing (bottom) is a brown tweed with more dark and light contrast. Mature caterpillars hibernate, and then pupate in the spring. The range of this butterfly reaches across Canada into the subarctic zone.

DOUG HEPBURN

DOUG HEPBURN

Propertius Duskywing   *Erynnis propertius*

Wingspan: 1⅜–1⅝ inches

Description: The **top** of the forewing is gray and brown, finely mottled in males and more coarsely mottled and browner in females. Several pale translucent spots are present on the forewing. The hindwing is brown.

Range in PNW: Cascade Mountains westward

Habitat: Deciduous forests

Host plant: Garry oak (*Quercus garryana*)

Female Propertius Duskywings (top right) stick round green eggs to the top of oak leaves. A male is shown at top left. The young caterpillars make nests either by bringing leaves together with silk strands or by cutting a channel around each side of a portion of a leaf, freeing it up so that it can be bent over and secured with silk. The caterpillars rest in these enclosures and eat nearby. Older caterpillars bind several leaves together into a nest. The caterpillars are yellowish with brown knobby heads. Most Propertius caterpillars hibernate, then form pupae in the spring.

Common Checkered Skipper   *Pyrgus communis*

Wingspan: 1–1¼ inches

Description: The wing fringes are checkered. The **top** is black with white squares coalesced into patches. The **underside** is golden gray crossed by shell-white bands.

Range in PNW: Oregon and eastern Washington into Idaho

Habitat: Meadows and disturbed weedy fields

Host plants: Species of mallow (*Malva*), including *M. rotundifolia*

When flying, Common Checkered Skippers look like fuzz balls caught by the wind and bounced along over the ground. Pale blue, faintly ribbed round eggs are laid on the top of mallow leaves, including the species that grows like a weed in lawns that are not meticulously groomed. Newborn caterpillars find a crease in the pleated leaves and pull the edges together as a secure refuge. Mature caterpillars leave the host plant and cover themselves with a silk net before pupating.

Two-banded Checkered Skipper   *Pyrgus ruralis*

Wingspan: ⅞–1⅛ inches

Description: The wing fringes are checkered. The **top** is black with white spots. The **underside** of the hindwing is brown tinted with copper and spotted with white like the top.

Range in PNW: Throughout, except treeless prairies

Habitat: Mountain meadows

Host plants: Species of *Potentilla*

The top of the Two-banded Checkered Skipper is mainly black with white spots that are discrete, not coalesced into patches. With a little imagination, my eye arranges the spots into a pair of parallel rows. The Two-banded Checkered Skipper is not as frequently seen as the Common Checkered Skipper and keeps more to remote mountain hideouts—typically, to moist meadows. If you're within sight of your car, chances are you're looking at the Common Checkered Skipper.

DOUG HEPBURN

Arctic Skipper *Carterocephalus palaemon*

Wingspan: 1–1¼ inches

Description: The **top** is dark brown with yellow-orange spots. The **underside** is golden copper with large oval pearl-colored spots rimmed by black.

Range in PNW: Coast Range, Cascade Mountains, Okanogan Highlands, Canada, and Idaho

Habitat: Forest openings and streamsides

Host plants: Species of grass (various genera), including *Calamagrostis purpurascens)*

This beautiful butterfly is unique enough to be recognized at once. The Arctic Skipper occurs throughout the coniferous forests of Canada and reaches into the forested mountains and foothills of the Pacific Northwest. It is not an alpine butterfly. Its habitat is like that of the Western Meadow Fritillary, and I have seen the two species together on the west side of the Cascade Mountains. Adults are on the wing in late spring and are typically seen on flowers or resting on foliage at the forest's edge. Arctic Skipper caterpillars are green with lighter stripes.

WILLIAM NEILL

DOUG HEPBURN

Juba Skipper   *Hesperia juba*

Wingspan: 1 ⅛–1 ⅜ inches

Description: The **top** is tawny orange with a brown band at the outer wing margins, scalloped inwardly; a brown streak runs diagonally across the forewing. The **underside** of the hindwing is tan or olive with square silver blotches.

Range in PNW: Throughout

Habitat: Many, including meadows, prairies, and urban gardens

Host plants: Grass species (various genera), including Kentucky bluegrass (*Poa pratensis*)

The Juba Skipper is common in arid, open country throughout the Pacific Northwest. There are two broods, with flights in the spring and early autumn. Like other skippers, the body is large in proportion to the wings. Hold one lightly between your fingers and you'll appreciate the strength of its flight muscles.

DOUG HEPBURN

WILLIAM NEILL

Woodland Skipper   *Ochlodes sylvanoides*

Wingspan: ⅞–1⅛ inches

Description: The **top** is tawny orange with a brown band at the outer wing margins, scalloped inwardly; a brown zigzag patch on the forewing runs diagonally from the basal area to the apex. The **underside** of the hindwing is tan or brown with square yellow patches.

Range in PNW: Throughout

Habitat: Many, including meadows, forest edges, and urban sites

Host plants: Species of grass (various genera), including wheatgrasses

Compared to the Juba Skipper, the Woodland Skipper is smaller and has rounder wings and a different, less distinct pattern on the underside. The underside can be darker than in the Woodland Skipper pictured here. The Woodland may be seen in almost any setting in our region. It comes to verbena and asters in my Portland garden in September. There is a spring brood and a fall brood, and the offspring of the latter hibernate as caterpillars.

DOUG HEPBURN

WILLIAM NEILL

Common Roadside Skipper   *Amblyscirtes vialis*

Wingspan: ⅞–1⅛ inches

Description: The wings are long and triangular, and the wing fringes are checkered. The **top** is dark brown with a cluster of white marks near the forewing apex. The **underside** is dark brown dusted with bluish violet on the outer third of the wings.

Range in PNW: Mountains east of Cascade Crest, and northern Coast Range of Oregon

Habitat: Moist mountain meadows

Host plants: Species of grass (various genera, including *Poa*)

The Common Roadside Skipper is at home in moist, sunny meadows surrounded by forest—especially meadows with streams. It has not been found over the broad area of the drier high desert and Columbia Basin. The one pictured here was at the edge of a dirt road that followed a stream through open mixed forest. The caterpillar is light green. The Common Roadside Skipper produces one brood per year, and adults fly in the spring and early summer.

DOUG HEPBURN

TELLING MALES FROM FEMALES

The distinction between genders is easy to make for some species; for others, it can be very difficult or impossible in the field. Here are some tips to use with butterflies of the Pacific Northwest.

Swallowtails: Males have a pair of flat claspers, one on each side at the tip of the abdomen. The space between them creates a cleft or slit, called the ventral slit, seen best from the underside. Yellow claspers are visible in the photo of a male Oregon Swallowtail on page 47 (left), one on each side of the lower tip of the abdomen, with a dark cleft between them.

Parnassians: Females that have copulated have a sphragis attached to their abdomen (see Clodius Parnassian, page 50). The female Mountain Parnassus is much darker than the male.

Whites: Males have a ventral slit near the tip of the abdomen. In the *Pieris* and *Neophasia* species, females have more black markings on the top surface.

Sulphurs: Males have a solid black band at the outer border of their wings; in females, the black is absent, attenuated, or invaded by yellow.

Coppers: The top of the wings is plain and usually iridescent in males; in females, it is spotted and not iridescent. The exception to this is the Lustrous Copper.

Hairstreaks and Elfins: Males have a small, sharply delineated oval scent pad near the center of the leading edge of their forewings. Exceptions to this are the Gray and Golden Hairstreaks.

Blues: The top surface of the wings is bright blue in males and darker blue or brown in females. An exception to this is the Arrowhead Blue.

Metalmarks: No obvious difference between males and females.

Fritillaries: Males have a ventral slit near the tip of the abdomen, most easily seen in members of the *Speyeria* genus.

Checkerspots: The forewing tip is more rounded in females.

Crescents: The pattern on the top surface of females' wings has greater contrast than the pattern on males' wings.

Anglewings and relatives: In the *Polygonia* species, males have more acutely indented wing margins and sharper underside patterns.

Aristocrats: In most of these species, it's not possible to determine gender in the field.

Browns: Females have a larger, rounder abdomen.

Skippers: No easy generalization.

GLOSSARY

Terms in this glossary are defined as they are used in this book.

abdomen. The posterior (rear) segment of the body, containing digestive, reproductive, and excretory organs.

adult. The final stage of the life cycle, when the insect possesses wings and is commonly thought of as a butterfly.

aedeagus. In insects, the male reproductive organ that introduces the spermatophore into females during copulation.

alpine. Descriptive of the biological zone in mountains above timberline, characterized by a brief summer and specialized low-growing plants.

anal angle. The sharply curved margin of the hindwing near the abdomen (see diagram, page 42).

antennae. A pair of long sensory appendages attached to the head; also known as feelers.

anterior. Situated toward the front or head.

apex. The tip of the forewing where costal and outer margins meet (see diagram, page 42).

arthropod. Any of a group of animals, or phylum, characterized in particular by jointed legs and exoskeletons.

basal area. The area of the wings adjacent to the body (see diagram, page 42).

basking. Posturing in sunshine to warm the body by absorbing radiant energy from the sun.

brood. A group of individuals of the same species that develop more or less simultaneously (in the same generation).

caterpillar. The larval form of a butterfly during its second stage of life, characterized by a wormlike shape, legs, and mandibles.

chrysalis. See **pupa**.

claspers. Small flat plates on each side at the tip of the abdomen in male butterflies. Used to grasp and stabilize the female's abdomen during copulation.

copulation. The physical contact between a male and female to introduce sperm into the female's body.

costal margin. The leading edge of the forewing (see diagram, page 42).

cross-fertilization. The transfer of pollen between different plants of the same species.

diapause. A dormant state in which the butterfly's activity and metabolism are greatly reduced.

egg. The first stage of a butterfly's life cycle, starting with a fertilized ovum, which grows into an embryo.

embryo. The primitive stage of an organism's development, characterized by rapid multiplication of cells and the formation of the basic body structure.

exoskeleton. The hard, supportive, protective outer shell of arthropods (including butterflies).

eyespot. A round mark, consisting of a central, pupil-like spot surrounded by one or more concentric rings, mimicking an eye.

fertilization. The combination of sperm and ovum resulting in a fertilized egg.

field mark. A physical feature useful for identifying a butterfly in the field.

forewing. Either of the pair of wings closest to the butterfly's head (see diagram, page 42).

genus (pl. genera). A group of closely related species; the genis is the first word (capitalized) of the binomial scientific name of a species.

habitat. The environment in which a species is typically found.

head. The anterior segment of the body, containing eyes, mouth, and antennae.

hemolymph. The fluid inside an insect's body that surrounds its organs and transports nutrients and hormones.

herb. A seed-producing plant without a permanent woody structure (for example, grasses and flowers).

hibernaculum. A tubular hibernation shelter that a caterpillar makes from a leaf remnant.

hindwing. Either of the pair of wings furthest from the butterfly's head (see diagram, page 42).

host plant. A species of plant used by a particular species of caterpillar for food.

insect. Any of a subset (class) of arthropods that have three pairs of jointed legs.

lateral. Located at or extending along the side.

larva (pl. larvae). The form some animals take during an early stage of development. Larvae of butterflies and moths are commonly known as caterpillars.

lepidoptera. Any of a subset (order) of insects that have scales on their wings. The order consists of butterflies and moths.

life cycle. The period of growth and maturation from egg through adult butterfly.

longitudinal. Extending lengthwise, along the long axis.

mandibles. Jaws for chewing.

meadow. Land, usually moist, where grasses and other herbs are the dominant plants.

metamorphosis. The change in physical form that occurs during the life cycle (egg, caterpillar, pupa, and adult).

montane. Descriptive of the biological zone below timberline in mountains, characterized by evergreen forest.

native plant. A plant originally occupying a particular area as opposed to one that is imported.

nectar. Fluid with high sugar concentration secreted by the nectary of a flower.

nectary. A gland in flowers that secretes nectar. Located between the base of the petals and the style.

ochre. Pale brownish yellow color.

ommatidium. The functional unit of a compound eye, consisting of its own lens, light receptors, and nerve connections.

osmeterium. The fleshy forked appendage of a swallowtail caterpillar that emits a pungent, sweet odor and protrudes from behind the caterpillar's head when it is alarmed (see Two-tailed Swallowtail species account, page 46).

outer margin. The edges of the wings, away from the body (see diagram, page 42).

overwinter. To live through the winter.

oviduct. The conduit between the exterior and the ovaries, serving as a passageway for eggs.

ovum. The reproductive cell of the female parent, which contains half the number of chromosomes present in an adult's cell; an unfertilized egg.

pheromone. A chemical used for communication between courting partners.

population. A group of individuals of the same species occurring in the same area.

posterior. Situated toward the back or behind.

prairie. Flat or rolling land with plants but few or no trees (usually due to limited water).

proboscis. A flexible feeding tube through which adult butterflies (and some other insects) suck liquids for nourishment.

proleg. A fleshy leg attached to an abdominal segment of a caterpillar.

pupa. The form a butterfly assumes in the third stage of its life cycle during its transition from caterpillar to adult.

range. The broad geographic distribution of a species.

reproductive capacity. The quantitative measure of an animal's potential for producing offspring; influenced by the number of eggs produced and the duration of the life cycle.

scent pad. The small, sharply delineated oval patch near the center of the leading edge of the forewings of many hairstreak species; emits pheromones believed to increase female receptivity to mating.

species. A group of individuals that mate with each other over successive generations.

sperm. The reproductive cell of a male parent, which contains half the number of chromosomes present in an adult's cell and can fertilize an ovum.

spermatophore. A packet of millions of sperm that is introduced into a female butterfly during copulation.

sphragis. A pale gray structure attached to the abdomen of a mated female parnassian butterfly. Her mate attaches it after copulation to prevent subsequent fertilization by another male.

subalpine. Descriptive of the transition zone between alpine and montane biological zones; includes features of both.

submarginal area. The area of the wing adjacent to the outer margin (see diagram, page 42).

subspecies. A subset of a species, usually reproductively isolated, with its own distinctive features.

thorax. The center segment of the body, which provides attachments for the legs and wings.

transverse. Situated across or crosswise. On a butterfly's wing, transverse marks run perpendicular to the wing veins.

ventral. Relating to or situated on the underside.

ventral slit. The linear space between the claspers at the tip of the abdomen in male butterflies.

wing veins. Firm linear struts that reinforce the wings (see diagram, page 42).

wing fringe. Hairlike structures at the outer margins of the wings.

wingspan. The distance between the tips of the forewings when extended horizontally with their trailing edges forming a straight line (see diagram, page 42).

SOURCES OF MORE INFORMATION

Brock, Jim P., and Kenn Kaufman. 2003. *Butterflies of North America*. New York: Houghton Mifflin Company.

Brown, F. M., D. Eff, and B. Rotger. 1957. *Colorado Butterflies*. Denver: Denver Museum of Natural History. (Black and white photos.)

Dornfeld, Ernst. 1980. *Butterflies of Oregon*. Forest Grove, OR: Timber Press. (Black and white photos; difficult to obtain.)

Ferris, C. D., and F. M. Brown. 2001. *Butterflies of the Rocky Mountain States*. Norman, OK: University of Oklahoma Press.

Glassberg, Jeffery. 2001. *Butterflies Through Binoculars: The West*. Oxford, UK: Oxford University Press.

Guppy, Crispin S., and Jon H. Shepard. 2001. *Butterflies of British Columbia*. Vancouver: University of British Columbia Press.

Hinchliff, John. 1994. *The Distribution of the Butterflies of Oregon*. Corvallis, OR: Oregon State University Bookstore, 1994. (Distribution maps only.)

Hinchliff, John. 1996. *The Distribution of the Butterflies of Washington*. Corvallis, OR.: Oregon State University Bookstore. (Distribution maps only.)

Miller, Jeffrey, and Paul C. Hammond. 2003. *Caterpillars and Adult Lepidoptera of Northwest Forests and Woodlands*. Morgantown, WV: U.S. Department of Agriculture, U.S. Forest Service.

Opler, Paul A., and Amy B. Wright. 1999. *Western Butterflies*. Peterson Field Guide Series. New York: Houghton Mifflin. (Covers North America west of the Great Plains and north of Mexico.)

Pyle, Robert M. 2002. *Butterflies of Cascadia*. Seattle, WA: Seattle Audubon Society.

Scott, James A. 1986. *Butterflies of North America*. Stanford, CA: Stanford University Press. (Especially good for natural history of butterflies.)

Xerces Society and Smithsonian Institution. 1990. *Butterfly Gardening*. San Francisco: Sierra Club Books.

INDEX